Where Should I Sit at Lunch?

The Ultimate 24/7 Guide to Surviving the High School Years

Harriet S. Mosatche, Ph.D., and Karen Unger, M.A.

McGraw-Hill

New York   Chicago   San Francisco   Lisbon   London   Madrid   Mexico City
Milan   New Delhi   San Juan   Seoul   Singapore   Sydney   Toronto

The *McGraw·Hill* Companies

Library of Congress Cataloging-in-Publication Data

Mosatche, Harriet S., 1949–
    Where should I sit at lunch? : the ultimate 24/7 guide to surviving the high school
years / by Harriet S. Mosatche and Karen Unger.
        p.   cm.
    ISBN 0-07-145928-6 (alk. paper)
        1. Teenagers—Life skills guides.   2. High school students—Life skills guides.
    I. Unger, Karen, 1954–   II. Title.

HQ796.M627   2006
646.700835—dc22   2005027002

1 2 3 4 5 6 7 8 9 0   FGR/FGR   0 9 8 7 6

ISBN 0-07-145928-6

Interior design by Think Design Group

McGraw-Hill books are available at special quantity discounts to use as premiums and
sales promotions, or for use in corporate training programs. For more information, please
write to the Director of Special Sales, Professional Publishing, McGraw-Hill, Two Penn
Plaza, New York, NY 10121-2298. Or contact your local bookstore.

This book is printed on acid-free paper.

To Ivan, Liz, and Rob with love.

—HSM

*To my mother, who shared her love of books,
and to my father, who always encouraged me to strive
to do the best I could. To my husband, who makes
it possible for me to realize my dreams, and
to my son, who is the best of me and much more.*

—KU

Contents

Preface

> Just before I entered high school, I was really nervous because I had heard all these horror stories about getting lost in the massive building. As soon as I entered the school, I remember everyone being helpful, and I was no longer scared. I did get lost in the building several times, but that happens to everyone. High school is a million times better than middle school. There is a ton more freedom and more people to meet, and you can choose some of your classes.

—ANDREW, 17

> Middle school was extremely difficult for me. I was teased a lot, and I didn't have many friends. The transition to high school was amazing. I immediately started making a ton of friends, and suddenly I had so many activities that I was part of. I *love* high school. I am so happy with my friends and what I do every day. I have never felt so confident.

—ELIZABETH, 16

> **"** If you make the right types of friends and do what you love, then your high school years should be amazing. **"**

—WENDY, 19

Welcome to High School Survival

Why are you reading this book? Are you a high school student looking for some advice? Are you reaching the end of middle school and curious as to what comes next?

High school is huge. Whether you live in a small town with a class of kids you've known since you were 6 or in a community where your middle school or junior high was local and you are heading to a regional high school of thousands, your high school years are very different from anything you have experienced before. In your high school years, you prepare—not only academically, but also socially, mentally, and emotionally—for the independence of the years to come.

Ten Tips to Get You Started

Dr. Jeff Matteson is the principal of Millbrook High School in New York. Here are his top ten tips (and, he adds, not in any order of importance) for success during the high school years:

1. **You have to just say no to some things.** You will find yourself chronically overbooked. You may want to be on everything. Schools with everything they offer to make "all" possible know you can't do it all. (See pages 167–69 for time management tips.)

2. **Find an adult mentor.** A teacher, coach, family friend, or librarian can help you focus your interests and energy and celebrate your successes. Find a mentor you can trust with your deepest confidences and most serious questions. (See pages 163–64 for guidance on how to find a mentor.)

3. **Show up.** Don't have a poor attendance record now—you wouldn't last at work if you did. You won't be successful in college either. It sounds simple, but it's important. Businesses look for good, talented people who show up—physically and mentally. (See pages 48–50 for ideas on managing stress so that you can stay focused.)

4. **Do the work.** Teachers really care. Teachers reward big time the kids who regularly do their homework. (See pages 138–42 for tips on teachers.)

5. **Communicate with your parents—for the most part, be open and honest.** (See pages 64–67 for how to do that.) Parents can't understand silence. Successful kids let their parents know what is going on. (See the advice from Stephen Wallace of SADD on pages 194–95.) You can still keep some stuff private, but give your parents a chance to understand your life.

6. **Stay safe, and know that your safety depends to a great extent upon yourself.** You don't have to be a "narc," but you do have to tell if you know that someone is planning to do something that will hurt others. (See pages 93–95.) Even an anonymous note is better than not telling when lives are at stake. Think about who you choose to get in a car with and what you are doing if you are self-medicating—you are not invincible.

7. **Get some sleep.** Computers are sleep burners. How much time do you waste? You can't think clearly and do well in

school if you are perpetually exhausted. (See pages 15–19 for ideas on staying healthy.)

8. **Set realistic personal goals.** (See pages 169–71 for goal-setting ideas.) Reflect on what you are good at and what others say you are good at. (See pages 31–32 on how to make a list.) What do people thank you for? That's probably what you are good at.

9. **Seek to make a difference.** Schools are like little cities. There are tons of opportunities to serve, not so you can get an award but so you can be a vital member of a community. You'll really grow as a human when you can help someone. (See pages 197–204 for ideas.)

10. **Figure out what you need and how you need to learn, and let your teachers know.** You have to be responsible for your own learning. (See pages 131–38.) Think about the teachers you liked best. Did they draw lots of pictures and diagrams? Give you lots of activity choices? Assign interesting projects? Have a great sense of humor? Your teachers and your schoolwork can help you figure out how you learn best.

> " Worry about yourself, not what everyone else is doing. Don't let anyone talk you into doing something you know is wrong. Do your work, stay focused, and just try to do your best. "
>
> —JULIA, 14

Bests and Worsts

What's the best thing about being in high school? The worst?

The best things about high school were the little things like the cafeteria's popcorn chicken, talking in the hallways, passing notes in class, watching girls walk down the hall with their skirts accidentally tucked into the back of their tights, leaving books in my friends' lockers if they were closer to my classroom, hanging out in the bathroom, the hilarious movies we had to watch in driver's ed, sneaking out of my assigned seat in the front of the classroom to go sit with my friends in the back, running to homeroom right before the last bell rang, eating Cocoa Puffs during English class . . . Basically my day-to-day activities that I never really regarded as anything special during high school are what I now really look back on and miss the most.

The worst part about high school is all the high school drama and B.S. that no one cares about as soon as you graduate. No one cares if you dated the homecoming king or that you were voted Nicest Hair in the yearbook. All of high school was basically a bunch of girls whining and crying about their terrible lives and going behind each other's backs and being mean to one another, and attitudes like that will get you nowhere in life, period. Guys are competitive and full of testosterone and always trying to outdo one another and be better than the next guy and funnier, and just like with girls, none of that will matter as soon as they are handed their diploma. So of these I have found some will grow up, but others seem to continue to have the maturity of a sophomore in high school, and they just have to get over themselves.

—WHITNEY, 19

“The best thing about high school was definitely my friends, 'cause I did a lot of fun stuff, hanging out, whatever. Regardless of the situation—we could have just been playing Ping Pong in my basement—it was the people I was with who made it fun. At the junior-year carnival, I rapped in front of three hundred people, and I'll never forget how awesome it felt when they rushed the stage, yelling for an encore. By senior year, everyone at school knew who I was—I had respect, I had a girlfriend, I knew what college I was going to, and I had a tight group of friends.

The worst thing about being in high school was the beginning of it. Every weekend, I would hang out with the same three guys, doing nothing. We didn't hang out with girls—that happened later. Freshman year was easy—we just had tons of boring busywork. But things got better, much better.”

—ROB, 19

About This Book

In *Where Should I Sit at Lunch? The Ultimate 24/7 Guide to Surviving the High School Years*, you'll find advice from experts: teens who have graduated from or who are in high school and professionals who work in many different fields. Why 24/7? Because this book doesn't just cover what happens during the school day, it covers all aspects of your high school life. You can read the book in order—or choose a chapter that answers a question you have now and then skip around. You may find it hard to believe that many people look back at high school as the best time of their lives. Or you may be so happy, you can't imagine what you will do once you graduate. Or—like most people—you may be somewhere in between. Wherever you fall on the love-hate high school spectrum, you'll find something in this book that will make your life better. And why is the title *Where Should I Sit at Lunch?* Because high school students said finding a group of kids they felt comfortable hanging out with was one of their biggest concerns when they first started high school. What about you?

Acknowledgments

Working with McGraw-Hill on this book has been an absolute joy. John Aherne, senior editor, has been consistently enthusiastic and encouraging. Thanks also to Susan Moore, Sarah Pelz, and the rest of the McGraw-Hill team. I am grateful to the experts who generously shared their knowledge and ideas with me: Audrey Jacobs Brockner, Sheryl Scalzo, Judy Strauss-Schwartz, Michael A. Tedesco, and Diane Tukman.

My children, Robert and Elizabeth, gave me valuable feedback and were constantly on call to find friends and acquaintances who would answer their mother's never-ending questions. My husband, Ivan Lawner, has always been totally supportive of my writing and is endlessly patient.

Many of my friends helped me locate teens who were willing to talk about their lives. The high school and college students across the country who shared their experiences made this book come alive for me. I truly appreciate their honesty, their insights, and their time.

—HSM

Thank you to McGraw-Hill for recognizing how tough the high school years can be, and its editors, John Aherne, who was the perfect combination of coach and wordsmith, and Susan Moore, who shepherded the manuscript to finish. A special thank-you to Sarah

Pelz for her hard work, enthusiasm, and creative suggestions. Thanks, too, to the design team, who created the teen-appealing look.

I cannot thank enough all of the experts, and the organizations and institutions they represent, who shared their experience and knowledge in these pages: Adam Aberman, Rick Beckwith, Maggie Blayney, Karen Bokram, Dr. Nancy Brown, Dr. Cheryl Dellasega, Danny McKeever, Trish Tchume, Stephen Wallace, Marlene Weber, Kelly Whalen, and Kelly White. Their advice is so much more useful and eloquent than mine would ever be.

Thank you to my friends who helped gather such insightful and real stories, but most of all, thank you to the high school and college students who gave such true-to-life and compelling quotes, especially those from Millbrook, Lyall Memorial Federated Church, Poughkeepsie Day School, and Stanford University. Their words are the heart of this book.

—KU

Body Stuff

 Physically, my self-image is of a short, rather heavy teen. I've got no trouble with the short part, but I do want to change the heavy part. I lost fifteen pounds in the past two years and am really proud of myself for that. I hope to lose another fifteen or more in the coming years, seeing as I still couldn't be called slender by any stretch of the imagination. I'd say I'm most self-conscious about my stomach, which always sticks out. **"**

—ANGELA, 16

Your Changing Body: The Wide Range of Normal

Your body has already gone through some of the big stuff. You know, a height growth spurt, a curvier or more muscular body, hair growing under your arms, and a lot of other changes. Maybe you had a tough time at the beginning because your shoe size and your body parts got larger overnight, and you just weren't ready. Or maybe you were the one who had to wait nervously for some sign that puberty had finally arrived, while your friends' body changes surged way ahead. Timing is a tough part of

1

puberty—some seventh-graders look like they're 19, while some 16-year-olds could still get into the movies at child prices.

Wherever you are on the road to physical maturity, you may be wondering what's normal. Basically, there's a very wide range. For girls, the first signs of puberty begin anywhere from 8 to 13, and for guys, anywhere from 10 to 15. That's why there was probably a time in middle school when you noticed some of the girls towering over a lot of the boys. High school is the time when boys play catch-up. If you're really worried about whether you're developing normally, talk to your doctor. But chances are, you're okay. Look at the following lists to see the specifics about puberty.

What Happens During Male Puberty?
➤ Height increases.
➤ Testicles and scrotum enlarge.
➤ Penis widens and lengthens.
➤ Pubic hair develops, gradually becoming curlier and darker.
➤ Facial and underarm hair develops.
➤ Voice deepens.
➤ Body and face mature.
➤ Leg hair becomes thicker and darker.
➤ Chest hair appears.
➤ First ejaculation occurs, typically in wet dreams (during sleep) or during masturbation.
➤ Erections are more frequent.
➤ Sweat glands are more active.
➤ Acne appears on face, chest, and back.

What Happens During Female Puberty?
➤ Height increases.
➤ Breasts develop.
➤ Underarm hair develops.
➤ Pubic hair develops, gradually becoming curlier and darker.
➤ Menstruation begins (cycle is often not regular for the first year or so).
➤ Leg hair gets thicker and darker.

- Thighs, hips, and buttocks fill out. (Most girls gain weight in those areas.)
- Sweat glands become more active.
- Acne appears on face, chest, and back (usually less severe than in boys).

Dozing in Class Doesn't Count as the Nine Hours of Sleep You Need

One thing that *isn't* changing is your need for sleep. The demands on your time are increasing, and you need at least as much sleep as you did during middle school. How are you going to fit everything in and still get enough sleep? Most high school students need about nine hours of sleep a night. Are you getting even close to that on an average school night? If you're sleep-deprived day after day, you can't focus very well on your schoolwork—or on anything else, for that matter. Unfortunately, most school schedules are out of sync with the physiology and sleep patterns of adolescents. You're feeling most alert in the evenings and most tired in the early morning hours— like at 8:30 in your American history class. Try establishing nightly routines that will help you fall asleep, which means no loud music, fights with parents, or intense IM conversations with friends around bedtime.

66 Basically, I never get enough sleep on school nights. I usually can't finish my homework before eleven, often later. I never get up in the morning before my CD alarm goes off, and even with loud music playing, it's hard to get out of bed. Most of the kids in my first-period class are in the same zombie state as me. 99

—BETH, 16

Body Basics and Beyond: Skin, Hair, Teeth, and Eyes

You've had your body for fourteen, fifteen, sixteen, or more years now, but do you take as good care of it as you should?

ZAPPING ZITS

So you've noticed that your skin is oilier than when you were a kid. Just when you're trying to impress that great-looking girl or guy, your face becomes a mass of nasty eruptions. What can you do about your pimples, which may not leave you until your college years, or maybe even later? In fact, throughout adulthood, lots of people experience periodic flare-ups of acne.

While you're waiting for your acne to subside, here are some tips:

➤ Don't obsess about your blemishes. Remind yourself that most people see the whole you and not your pimples.
➤ Use a cleanser recommended for oily skin, and use it often—or at least morning and night. And don't forget your chest and back, particularly you guys. Girls, no matter how tired you are, never go to bed with your makeup on. If your skin gets too dry from a particular cleanser, try a different brand.
➤ Tempted as you are, don't pick at your pimples. And avoid touching your face.
➤ Drink lots of water, and eat healthy food. Although most experts don't think food plays a significant role in your complexion, the rest of your body won't mind a decent diet.
➤ See a dermatologist if the condition of your skin really bothers you or if your zits seem particularly inflamed. Your doctor can prescribe antibiotics and special creams. Once you get them, you just have to remember to follow directions and use them religiously.

Expert Skin Care Advice

Marlene Weber, the owner of two day spas in the Hudson Valley region of New York, has also managed the salon at Bloomingdale's in New York City; styled hair and makeup for fashion magazines, including Cosmopolitan *and* Vogue, *television, and film; and worked as a national trainer and artist for Aveda, L'Oréal, and Clairol. She and her staff offer this skin care advice.*

The bad news is most teens will have some form of acne. The good news is you have many options: over-the-counter preparations, visits to an esthetician (a licensed skin care professional), and medical direction from a board-certified dermatologist (a medical doctor who specializes in skin disorders). Acne treatment begins by washing your face gently. Don't scrub, because you can open the blemish and spread the bacteria in the pimples. Cleanse using a fresh pad or a natural facial sponge that can be washed. Use something clean or new on your face, so you don't re-infect your skin. Wash away surface oils with a non-oily cleansing cream or gel. Use a product with salicylic acid, hyaluronic acid, or benzoyl peroxide to treat.

If you play sports, work in a humid environment, or do other activities that make you sweat, wash your face more often or carry non-oily cleansing wipes. Don't squeeze or pick your pimples—that can make the infection worse. Change your pillowcase frequently. Keep your hair clean and off your face.

You can seek the advice of an esthetician your doctor recommends or at a skin care salon. If you're scheduling an appointment on your own, make sure you ask for a licensed esthetician who specializes in teenage acne treatment. The esthetician should analyze your skin under a magnifying lamp and recommend a skin care routine. Know that changing your skin's appearance takes time, so you have to be patient. A board-certified dermatologist can recommend antibiotics or other medications. Know that these drugs may have side effects, some of which are quite severe.

Hair Dos . . . and Don'ts

The oil that's playing havoc with your skin is also greasing up your hair. That means you need to wash often—every day might be necessary if you've got particularly oily hair—and maybe use a shampoo formulated for your hair type. But if you've noticed dandruff flakes or if your hair tends to be dry, find a shampoo that's right for those problems. While shampoo directions tell you to lather twice, don't bother. Your hair gets clean enough from one round. Experiment with other kinds of hair products, like rinses, conditioners, and gels, to see which ones are worth the expense.

How do you know what kind of hairstyle works for you? Ask your friends—your real friends, not the ones who major in jealousy. Experiment with different looks. And that's not just a suggestion for the girls. Guys, too, can have fun with their hair. Wearing hair the same way year after year gets boring. With certain computer programs, you can even see what you'd look like with a different hairstyle without risking a single lock of your hair.

Sitting in the chair, waiting for a haircut? Tell your hairstylist what you want. If you leave it vague ("just make me look good"), you may end up very unhappy. As soon as you notice things going astray—the stylist is about to cut what looks like a big chunk from one side of your head—calmly but quickly say, "No, that's not what I want." Remember, it's your hair and your money. Don't be timid; assert yourself.

> Once in a while, I have my hair highlighted blond—it's naturally light brown. I get bored with the same look. And for the same reason, I change the length of my hair from time to time. My cycle is this: I let it grow out and then get sick of having to spend so much time taking care of it. I then get it cut extremely short. After about two years of that, I get bored by the fact that I can't play with it, and I begin to grow it again.

— SAMANTHA, 16

Care for Your Teeth

Lots of high school students wear braces. Some started wearing them in middle school, others not until high school. Timing partly depends on when you lose all your baby teeth. Still others wear braces for a year or two, wear a retainer for a couple of years, and then back to braces again. If you have to continue wearing braces for a while in college, you won't be the only one.

You have lots of braces options. Some are not as obvious as others, but the ones that are less visible usually cost more and may be more fragile, which means more trips to the orthodontist for repairs. While your braces are on, be extra conscientious about brushing and flossing.

> I've always looked young for my age. When I was 14, I was mistaken for an 11-year-old by a waitress who thought I should get the kids' price on the buffet. As I've gotten older, it's happened less often. But about a month ago, I got braces, and when I looked in the mirror, the first thing I noticed wasn't the braces, but the fact that once again I looked like a 12-year-old. I could deal with my friends teasing me about my getting braces in my junior year of high school, but I hated looking so young. For a couple of days, I tried not smiling too much, but that wasn't very practical, and for two weeks after getting my braces, I wore makeup every day to school, so I would look at least 14. Finally, I figured out that the people who matter know how old I am, so I'm more relaxed about my appearance now.
>
> —LIZ, 16

Even if you don't have braces, it's a good idea to brush and floss regularly to prevent tooth decay and infection. If you've never had sealants put on your teeth, ask your dentist about them; these coatings offer protection against decay.

You may have to deal with wisdom teeth. Some people don't have them, or they break through the gums without a fuss. But for other people, wisdom teeth can be impacted, which means they are blocked by another tooth, or even surrounding bone or gum tissue, from getting into the correct position. When that happens, they often have to be pulled.

Some of your friends might have their teeth professionally whitened or use over-the-counter whitening strips or gels. The American Dental Association's general recommendation is that you wait until you're 16 to have your teeth whitened, because that is when tooth enamel is fully formed. If your teeth have matured at a younger age, the process may be okay at 14 or 15, but it's always best to check with your dentist, who knows your particular teeth and which products are the safest and most effective.

> I used those strips, but probably not long enough for them to work, because they tasted bad and I didn't have the time for it.
>
> —PAOLA, 16

> I got my teeth whitened with a laser technique over winter break. It made my teeth sooooo white!! They were almost off the charts of whiteness!
>
> —MEGHAN, 19

*When it comes to taking care of your
eyes, Judy Strauss-Schwartz, M.Ed., is an expert.
She's a teacher of the visually impaired and adjunct
instructor in a program for teachers of students who are blind or
visually impaired. Here's her advice.*

Whether you need glasses or not, it's important for everyone to protect their eyes against the ultraviolet rays of the sun. Over time, the amount of damage to the eye increases and can lead to visual impairment. Don't buy a pair of sunglasses just because they're cool—make sure the sunglasses have 100 percent UV protection.

SQUINTING AT THE BOARD? YOU GOTTA SEE TO PASS YOUR ROAD TEST

If you've been wearing glasses since you were 7, they're probably not an issue for you. But if you find out in high school that you need glasses (maybe you finally figured out that you were the only one sitting in the third row who couldn't make out the chemistry formula on the board), then you've got to adjust a little. Even if you decide to go with contact lenses, you'll still need to wear glasses from time to time—like when you oversleep and have exactly four minutes to get ready for school or when you have a bad allergy attack with runny eyes. Some people can't wear contacts very often for medical reasons or can't wear them for long periods. And some just don't want to be bothered.

Glasses come in attractive colors and styles. Some people think of glasses as fashion accessories, and they match their glasses to their outfits or their moods. When you order glasses, ask for lenses that block out ultraviolet light.

Decorating Your Body: Makeup, Hair Color, Piercing, and Tattoos

The day proper little Janine comes into school with a gold hoop sticking out of her navel right below the bottom of that cropped red T-shirt is the day people may see her differently. Has she rebelled, gone wild, or just maybe discovered that she likes this new look? Makeup, body piercings, tattoos, and a different hair color can change your appearance and the way others perceive you. But some carry risks that you should know about.

THE ALLURE OF MAKEUP

Not many guys use makeup, so this section is mainly for girls. Here are some makeup tips for those who like using it. And for those who don't, enjoy your natural look.

> I almost never wear makeup. Once in a while, when going to a party, performing in a band concert, or for some other special occasion, I use lipstick, eye shadow, and blush sparingly. I use it because I like how it looks, though it's too much of a pain to use regularly. I used the most makeup when I was 13 and had twelve bar and bat mitzvahs of my peers to attend.
>
> —SAMANTHA, 16

> I started wearing makeup occasionally in sixth grade and started wearing a little every day in eighth grade. Now, on a normal school day, I usually only have time to put on eyeliner

Tips for Making Up

➤ Don't share makeup,
  particularly eye makeup and lipsticks, even with your
  closest friends, or you might end up sharing infections.
➤ Remember that less is more. Too much makeup often looks
  strange, rather than attractive. Unless it's Halloween or you're
  going to be on TV, go for makeup that's natural looking. Take
  note of when people compliment you on your appearance. What
  kind of cosmetics were you using?
➤ Use a concealer to cover up blemishes. Find one that's formulated to hide and heal pimples.
➤ If you wear foundation, get one that has an SPF rating. You're
  not too young to protect your skin from the sun's rays.
➤ Have fun with makeup. Some days you can wear more, other
  days less or none. If you wear eyeliner, mascara, eye shadow,
  brow liner, foundation, blush, lip liner, and lipstick every single
  day, you'll panic the morning you get up late and have to make
  the choice between missing your math class and putting on
  makeup.
➤ Nothing lasts forever, including your makeup. Once you've
  opened it, get rid of eye makeup in three months, foundation
  and lipstick after six months. And any time makeup doesn't look
  right or has a strange odor, get rid of it right away—you might be
  smelling bacteria growing.

and lip gloss. If I'm going out, I try to put on
a little more. I wear makeup to look at least
semi-presentable and fix up any little
problems I see.

—AMY, 16

Hair-Raising Tips

Maybe you're a brunette who wants to be blond. Or you're intrigued by the red-hair craze. If you just want to have fun with a radically different look, you could spray your hair with that temporary blue, green, or red stuff and then wash it out. But if you're seriously thinking about coloring your hair, here are some things to keep in mind:

➤ Your natural hair color is uniquely yours, which means that when you dye your hair, the color may not be exactly as pictured on the box.

➤ Hair dye comes in three basic levels from one that gradually washes out in about two dozen shampoos to those that are permanent.

➤ Permanent hair color, often called Level 3, really is permanent, which means it stays in until your hair grows out—think black roots on a blonde head—or until you dye your hair or your roots.

➤ Hair dye is a chemical, so seriously consider the precautions described on the hair color box. Dyed hair will not have the same texture as natural hair, since it's been chemically altered.

> I dyed my hair blue once. I kinda liked change, so you know it was entertaining. It wasn't really a rebellious-phase thing.

—GABE, 16

> I get my hair highlighted two or three times a year, just 'cause I like it and 'cause my black hair makes me look too old and the hair looks extra greasy.

—WENDY, 19

A Hole Lotta Piercing Going On

Is a hole or two in your earlobe not enough? Multiple earlobe piercings are common, as are piercings of other body parts. But anything that pierces the skin can potentially spread infection, such as HIV, hepatitis, and penicillin-resistant bacteria. So before you get that tiny barbell implanted in your navel, make sure that the piercing facility is spotless and that the person doing the piercing is following safety procedures. Your skin and the instruments must both be disinfected.

The list of complications of nipple, navel, tongue, and genital piercing is long. In some cases, stud earrings have become embedded in the skin as if the body had been trying to heal over an injury, and clothing can easily catch on a jeweled navel, causing tears and infection. Nipple rings that go too deep might damage breast tissue and later lead to problems in breast-feeding. Tongue rings are particularly problematic, since every movement of the tongue causes the jewelry to knock against the teeth. In time, a tooth can get chipped or broken, requiring expensive and time-consuming tooth restoration or even replacement.

If you have piercings that you'd like closed up, simply take out the jewelry and wait. In time, most will close up with little or no scarring.

> **"** I have my ears pierced: two on the left one and three on the right. I just liked them, so I got them. **"**

—WENDY, 19

Wearing Your Heart on Your Bicep

Tattoos have become more commonplace among high school and college students. If your heart is set on getting a tattoo and your parents don't object to it, remember that tattoos are permanent. Pick a design that you'll be able to live with in five years or even twenty.

Remember, too, that a tattoo you get on young skin and a teen body may look very different twenty or more years later. Tattoo removal is incredibly complicated, requiring laser treatments to break down the ink pigment. And the removal process is expensive and time-consuming—sometimes taking weeks. Most important is making sure that the tattoo artist uses a new needle and fresh ink from sealed, disposable containers.

> "I have a tattoo on my arm: my name with a rose under it. I got it when I was 18 because I thought it was cute at the time. Now I realize I didn't need it because I'm cute without it, and all it did was damage my skin."
>
> —JULIA, 20

How Thin Do You Think You Look? Options for Change

Changing the way you eat and upping your exercise habit can be positive ways to change the way you look and feel, unless your behavior becomes extreme.

> "When I wear jeans and a tight shirt, I get self-conscious because then my love handles are noticeable. You can be thin and have love handles, which make you look fat, even though you're really not."
>
> —PAOLA, 16

> **"** I'm big and I'm beautiful. I wouldn't change
> anything, because I love me. **"**

—JULIA, 20

FOCUS ON FOOD

You see a perfect-looking model in a magazine or a movie star with six-pack abs, and you think to yourself: that will never be me. Everyone has felt that way at one time or another. Probably no one is ever completely satisfied with their shape and size, but it's easier to work at feeling good about how you do look—your self-image—than to rework your whole body into some kind of "ideal" that may be pretty near impossible to achieve.

You may be able to get away with a steady diet of soft drinks and fries for now, but does your body really want—or need—that? What you eat is about more than weight; it's about feeling good and having energy. If you are overweight, you can modify your diet and exercise regimen. Check with your doctor to find out the appropriate weight for you. While your friends and parents probably have an opinion on the subject, they're not completely objective sources.

Obesity, an increasing problem at all ages, is generally defined as being 20 percent over your normal weight range. Research needs to discover all the underlying factors, but likely causes include genetic predispositions (this is something you can, at least, partly blame on your family), overeating, inadequate physical activity, and hormonal conditions. Even sleep deprivation can play a role. People tend to eat more when they're tired, and statistics show teens are often sleep deprived.

You probably know what a sensible diet is, but sticking to it is a different matter. The following list gives you some ideas to get you started.

Ideas for Healthy Eating

➤ Eat breakfast. You'll be less
  hungry later in the day and less likely to overeat.
➤ Don't resort to fad diets. It's too hard to stick to them
  for the long haul.
➤ Increase your physical activity. Your metabolism will increase, so
  you'll be burning those calories more quickly.
➤ If you're a vegetarian, check with a doctor or nutritionist to make
  sure you're getting all the nutrients you need.
➤ Eat a variety of foods, but pay attention to portions. Most people
  overestimate what a single serving size looks like. A serving size,
  for example, is half a bagel or three ounces of cooked chicken
  (about the size of a deck of cards).
➤ Don't deprive yourself of the food you love, like ice cream, but
  eat smaller portions—a scoop instead of a carton. In the long
  run, feeling deprived will just lead to overindulging when you
  have the chance.

According to the American Heart Association, 5.3 million kids between 12 and 19 are overweight or obese. Obesity is more than a physical problem. The social isolation, embarrassment, and sense of hopelessness that you might face are sometimes more difficult to deal with than the physical effects. If you're very overweight, you have to think twice before doing lots of ordinary things. Will you be able to fit into the seat at the movies or at a sports arena? Will people be whispering behind your back when you order even a small ice-cream cone?

I was on a diet right before my boyfriend's prom because I needed to fit comfortably into my dress. But then I gained the weight back. I was happy when I lost it but then was really upset when I gained it back. During the school year, I have a lot of stress and I'm not quite as active, so it's hard not to gain weight. **"**

—PAM, 16

" When I was in middle school, I had low self-esteem because I was big. I was mad because I was the tallest girl in my class. And I felt that my breasts were too big. But in high school, I learned to appreciate and love myself. **"**

—MONICA, 19

TREATING OBESITY WITH SURGERY

When faced with extreme obesity as well as other health problems, such as type 2 diabetes and high blood pressure, some teens have turned to gastric bypass surgery. The operation involves stapling off a large section of the stomach and reducing the size of the small intestines. Afterward, people can eat only about half a cup of food at one time—for life. While some doctors think that teens are too young emotionally and physically to deal with the surgery, others say that for those teens suffering from dangerous health conditions, the gastric bypass offers an opportunity for a healthier life.

GET MOVING

Do you exercise regularly? If you're on a sports team, you probably do, but what happens during off-season? Do you take dance classes or jog? Those certainly count as physical activity. In 2003, according to the International Health, Racquet and Sportsclub Association, 4.5 million gym members were under the age of 18, so you might be among the teens getting your workouts at a club. Exercise doesn't have to mean Pilates or spinning classes, although those can be fun. What's really important is fitting some combination of strength, endurance, and flexibility workouts into your life on a regular basis—and that doesn't mean one weekend a month. Most experts suggest at least thirty minutes of exercise three or more days a week.

Why bother getting fit? Not only will you feel better during your high school years, but physical activity is also a habit that you'll benefit from your whole life—building muscles and decreasing your risk of obesity, high blood pressure, and heart conditions. Don't forget about the positive impact of exercise on your mental health. Physical activity reduces stress and increases your self-confidence. Ready to go running yet?

If you've been a real couch potato, you'd better check with your doctor before you start training for a marathon. But when you're ready to include physical activity in your life, keep in mind the following tips.

Tips for a Healthy Workout

➤ Drink lots of water—before, during, and after your workout—no matter what the weather, particularly when you're sweating a lot. But don't overdo; there is such a thing as too much water.

➤ Layer your clothing, so you can remove some as you begin to warm up.

➤ If you're exercising outside, prepare for the weather. Running at high noon when it's ninety-five degrees with intense humidity is not smart. Nor is running in icy temperatures without warm gloves or mittens and a hat.

➤ Wear properly fitting shoes of the right type for the activity. You'll feel more comfortable, perform better, and prevent injuries.

> Stretch after you've warmed up a bit. That means jog slowly, ride a bike, or even march in place while making circles with your arms for a few minutes before you start stretching your muscles.
> Don't do the same set of activities every single day. Your body needs time to heal before the next workout.
> Include strength training or weight lifting in your workout. That's not just for your appearance, although a toned body does look good. Strength training not only builds muscles around your joints and bone mass, but also increases the efficiency with which your body uses fat.
> Listen to your body. Slow down or even stop exercising for a few days when you feel sick or really sore. Once you're feeling up to it, you'll be back to your regular routine in no time.

" Over the summer I gained about seven pounds in muscle, and considering I was pretty darn skinny before, it felt good. I started exercising to keep up with basketball. Because of my height, I usually play a forward position, so I needed the weight to play that position. I had been working out seven days a week for the summer, and I felt like I had accomplished something. But when school came, I didn't have that kind of time, so now I just work out whenever I get the chance. "

—GABE, 16

Hate the Nose You Were Born With?

In 2003, about 225,000 young people ages 18 and under had cosmetic procedures, with about 39,000 of them surgical procedures. High as these numbers are, they're expected to continue to rise. Why?

Reality TV shows depicting extreme body transformations probably have something to do with it. But what you see in a one-hour show doesn't even begin to demonstrate the painful reality of recovery from these operations. And those candidates have been thoroughly investigated and prepped before any surgery begins, and they're totally pampered afterward.

Long before these shows were put on the air, people have wanted to alter their appearance. Rhinoplasties ("nose jobs") are nothing new, but more and more teens are also opting for breast reduction (done on males as well as females), liposuction (removing pockets of fat), otoplasty (pinning back the ears), and dermabrasion (a procedure that reduces acne scars). Plastic surgery falls into two basic categories. Reconstructive is for repairing significant defects, such as birth defects or injuries from burns, car accidents, or other traumas. Cosmetic procedures, the second type, are performed because people are not happy with their appearance.

Any reputable plastic surgeon will spend a lot of time interviewing people in your age group to decide if they are truly good candidates. Are you physically ready and emotionally mature enough to handle not just the surgery, but the recovery and the psychological aftereffects? Some teens suffer from body dysmorphia disorder (BDD), which means that no matter what they do to their appearance, they just can't be happy with how they look. They might turn to unnecessary plastic surgery or other drastic measures because they magnify flaws that others barely notice. Surgery is not the answer for them, but they do need some kind of professional help to deal with a serious problem with their body image. Sixteen is the average age for BDD to show up.

The summer between the end of high school and the beginning of college is a common time for teens to opt for a cosmetic procedure—a new look for a new life phase. If you're considering any kind of plastic surgery, think long and hard about why you feel like you need it. Also, your body is still changing: a feature that looks too large or too small now may look fine in a couple of years. Almost everyone is self-conscious and would like some aspect of their appearance to be different. Are you trying to meet someone else's idea of attractiveness or trying to fit in? Think of easier, safer, and far cheaper ways to accomplish that. And keep in mind the risks of surgery. Anesthesia carries with it some risk, small though it may be, of blood clots, heart attacks, strokes, injury to the brain, and even death. A surgeon might accidentally cut a nerve, causing numbness. And sometimes the outcome is downright unattractive, even requiring a second surgery to fix what's been botched in the first one.

Doctors: When Do You Need Them?

While you have lots of information available to make good decisions on your own or with the help of your family, sometimes you might be faced with situations that call for professional help. Your doctor can answer questions you might have about your body and can also refer you to other professionals, such as psychologists or surgeons if that's warranted.

EATING DISORDERS

High school girls and increasingly boys are often terrified of being overweight. The shape you might think of as being ideal is unattainable for most anybody. If you or your friends develop eating disorders, you need professional intervention—and fast. This is serious business. Untreated, eating disorders result in devastating illnesses, even death. Is this meant to scare you? Yes, if you or your friends are showing signs of anorexia nervosa (called anorexia for short), bulimia nervosa (usually just called bulimia), or binge eating—the major eating disorders. Anorexia and bulimia are both dangerous and life-threatening disorders. Chemical imbalances can occur that lead to problems with digestion, kidney function, and even complete heart failure. Eating disorders have the highest fatality rate of any mental illness.

Signs of an Eating Disorder

Symptoms of Anorexia Nervosa
- ➤ Starvation diet
- ➤ Avoidance of food and/or food rituals
- ➤ Unrealistic body image, believing she/he is not thin enough
- ➤ Often begins with a diet
- ➤ Perception of weight loss as an achievement
- ➤ Loss of hair or dull, dry hair
- ➤ Sensitivity to the cold
- ➤ Absence of menstruation

Symptoms of Bulimia Nervosa
- ➤ Binge eating followed by purging (throwing up, using laxatives, exercising excessively, or fasting)
- ➤ Often secret eating
- ➤ Obsession with food, weight, and appearance
- ➤ Dental problems, including tooth decay, damage to tooth enamel, and gum disease
- ➤ Irregular or absence of menstruation
- ➤ Making excuses about using the bathroom right after meals

Symptoms of Binge Eating Disorder
- ➤ Repeated episodes of binge eating
- ➤ Binge eating not followed by purging, fasting, excessive exercising, or other ways to compensate for the large amount of food ingested
- ➤ Guilt and depression associated with binge eating
- ➤ Lack of control over eating

I flirted with anorexia when I was 12, which lasted for about four or five months, although I frequently crash-dieted for the next four years. My family didn't know about it. I got lectured for not eating, but I always made excuses, saying I ate a lot for lunch or had lots of after-school snacks. My friends knew, and I got yelled at a lot during lunch. There were plenty of comments about how I was thin enough and needed to gain weight. My best friend and I, who were doing the same thing, made a game of it. This sharing made us deny that it was a problem. We would compare who ate less and who lost more weight. She would brag about winning every time because she weighed more than me to begin with.

I got over my eating disorder, mainly because I started figure skating, which requires lots of calories for strength and energy. I had a hard time jumping when I didn't eat. Then in my junior year of high school, I dated this guy who made me believe I would never be smart, thin, or pretty enough for him, so I put myself on lots of exercise and reduced calories for two months before the prom. All during high school, I would flip out every time I gained weight. My advice to high school students with eating disorders: weight is only a number; what matters is how healthy you are.

—JENNY, 19

I have a friend who is anorexic. She's a 'workout queen' and lost a ton of weight over winter break. She's the type of person who puts others in front of herself, so she always says she's 'fine' and will be 'fine.' But we all know that isn't true, because she has a bad self-image.

—MEGHAN, 19

VISITING A GYNECOLOGIST

If you're a guy, this is a section you can skip, unless you're curious or want to have a better understanding of what girls deal with. If you're a girl in high school, you should consider visiting a gynecologist under any of the following circumstances: you're sexually active, you're thinking of becoming so, you have symptoms of a vaginal infection (such as an unusual discharge), you're 16 and haven't started menstruating yet, your family has a history of ovarian cancer, or just because you're 18.

Before your first visit, talk to someone who has been there, so you know what to expect. And going to the gynecologist is something you should start getting used to—once you turn 18, it should be something you do every year! The doctor will take a fairly detailed medical history. Go to the appointment prepared with any questions you may have. Try not to feel too self-conscious and anxious. Your gynecologist will probably do a breast exam, take your blood pressure, and weigh you, along with doing a pelvic exam. You lie down on a table and insert your feet into stirrups to allow the doctor to check your vagina using a gloved finger and a speculum, a special instrument that pushes back the walls of the vagina. The more you can relax, the easier the exam will be, and it takes a very short time—just a few minutes. As part of the exam, your gynecologist will do a Pap smear, collecting cell samples from the cervix—the lower part of the uterus at the top of the vagina—with a cotton swab to check for abnormalities (which, by the way, are very rare). It's a good idea to get one of these tests done annually. Depending on the reason for your visit, you might also need to give a blood sample, which can uncover any hormonal imbalances.

Looking Ahead

Your high school years are a great time to start some habits that will work for you throughout your life, like walking instead of driving whenever you can and making healthy food choices most of the time. What can you start doing today?

The Inner You

> " It's really hitting me now that my summer is almost over. I just feel like this summer was disappointing. Sure, there were some good parts, some cool, fun things that happened, but on the whole it just wasn't what I'd been hoping for—no truly amazing parties, no summer fling . . . I'm sure that once school starts again, I'll be enjoying the new year at school, but for now, I feel kind of sad. "

—ANDY, 17

Underneath It All, Are You Happy?

You've got a lot going on in your life right now—harder classes than ever before, maybe a relationship that's going nowhere when you want it to go somewhere, or vice versa, conflicts with your parents over everything from curfews to privacy issues. Throw in the stress of college applications in the not-too-distant future and friends going through their personal nightmares, and you've got your hands emotionally full. Where does the needle on your feelings meter register? Are you overwhelmed but basically happy? Are you hiding out in your room, too depressed to face your friends? Are you just not sure, since your feelings are changing from one moment to the next? Your brain is different from the kid brain or the adult one—that's part of the reason why you're probably experiencing some pretty extreme emotional states.

YOUR HAPPINESS QUOTIENT

Complete these sentences to get a better sense of your happiness quotient and what's behind it.

1. I feel happiest when I _____

_____.

2. When I'm with _____, I usually feel happy.

3. When I'm not happy, I try to _____

_____.

4. I was happiest at the age of _____, because _____

_____.

5. In terms of happiness, my friends typically think of me as _____

_____.

6. In terms of happiness, family members usually see me as _____

_____.

7. When something goes wrong in my life, I _____

_____.

8. When something goes right in my life, I _____

_____.

" I consider myself to be very happy. I'm happiest in school either when I'm in a class where I'm actually learning something—don't laugh, most of my teachers can't teach—or when I'm at home chatting with a couple of friends or relaxing. **"**

—TANEISHA, 16

" I'm always outwardly happy, but at home, I show my true feelings. When I'm upset, I don't show it in public. **"**

—ISABELLA, 16

" My happiest time in high school was in my senior year from spring break until I went off to college. Everything was going well for me then. I had a very nice and pretty girlfriend, school was easy and I didn't really have or do any work, and I had plenty of friends to hang out with all the time. **"**

—KEITH, 19

FEEL GOOD ABOUT WHO YOU ARE

You may not know it, but you've been working on your identity—who you are, what you value, and where you're going in life—for a long time. While your image of yourself is sure to change throughout adulthood, you're beginning to settle into one way of seeing yourself. Are you the first to try every fad that comes along or the one who waits to see what everyone else is doing or wearing? Do you love being in the spotlight or playing behind the scenes? Are you the friend everyone goes to for advice or the one who shares the latest gossip? Or both? Whatever your qualities, you'll feel best if you're comfortable with who you are.

> " I stay true to what I believe. Popular fashions, thoughts, and positions cannot sway me to change. "
>
> —SAMANTHA, 16

> " I can socialize with more or less anybody. Like I have a rather diverse group of friends. I'm comfortable in most situations. "
>
> —GABE, 16

> " My sense of responsibility has made me successful thus far in life, whether it has to do with academics, extracurriculars, or social activities. "
>
> —FAIQA, 19

Take an inventory of your personal characteristics—the good and the not-so-good. Think about what you want to change, if anything, and then put together a makeover plan. The Personal Inventory Chart guides you through the steps.

Personal Inventory Chart

List your top five personal qualities—what you really like about you.

1. _____

2. _____

3. _____

4. _____

5. _____

Celebrate those high fives!

List your bottom five personal qualities—what you really don't like about you.

1. _____

2. _____

3. _____

4. _____

5. _____

Choose one of the bottom five qualities you most want to change.

_____

Describe what you would be like if you eliminated that quality from your life or pushed it in a more positive direction.

_____

_____

_____

Write five small (be realistic) steps you can take to get you from awful to awesome in that one quality.

1. _____

2. _____

3. _____

4. _____

5. _____

Next to each of those steps, write a date. Think of each of those dates as deadlines, like when you're writing a term paper. You now have the outline of a real plan. Go for it! (For more detailed information on setting goals, see pages 169–71.)

Dealing with Life's Negatives: Anger, Grief, and Depression

While you might have been protected from some of the negatives when you were younger, no one gets through the high school years without some emotional pain. Undoubtedly, you will face some situations that will make you angry or sad. While you can't avoid every tough spot, you can develop skills that will help you meet these challenges. Finding people who will come through for you during those difficult times is a good idea. (See pages 163–64 for tips on finding a mentor.)

Being funny has been one of my lifelong traits. It's a coping mechanism. Whenever I'm feeling down or overwhelmed, making a joke puts me into a better mood, and it makes everyone else laugh.

—DANIELLE, 16

COPING WITH ANGER

What's your anger style? Everyone has a distinct way of feeling and showing anger. At one end are those who keep their emotions so bottled up inside that no one even realizes something's wrong. At the other end are those who explode on such a grand scale that no one could miss the fireworks. What makes you furious will differ, too. You might wonder how one friend stayed so calm in a situation where you lost control, while another friend might be thinking about your ability to stay cool when she went ballistic. You might show your anger in subtle and different ways. For example, if you're angry with a parent, you might start screwing up in school or "forgetting" to call when you're going to be late.

I get angry a lot, but not many people realize it. I guess what makes me angry is if people let me down in some way, like if they cancel plans at the last minute, or if they are really late to something without even saying 'sorry' or acknowledging that I waited for them.

—L'QUON, 16

> **"** When I'm angry or frustrated at home, I like to be left alone. Otherwise, I'll just snap at my family. Once when I was really angry, I hit the wall. And then I thought, 'That was a bad idea.' I don't know why people in the movies always do that. It hurts your hand. **"**

—EILEEN, 16

> **"** I usually get angry when someone has said or done something that is rude or inconsiderate. I usually tell the person and give them an attitude until I'm not mad anymore or they apologize. **"**

—LIN-YEE, 19

If your anger has become your best friend and you can't let it go, it's time to find healthier outlets for your emotions. Holding onto anger hurts you physically (think about how your body feels when you are angry), mentally (it's hard to focus on anything else when you're all wrapped up in your anger), and socially (how many people really want to hang around with someone who's always angry?). Here are some suggestions for coping with your anger:

➤ Work out—the more strenuous, the better.
➤ Listen to music.
➤ Write about your feelings in a journal. You may finish writing about an episode and recognize that you've gotten worked up over basically nothing—or not. Then you can write about what to do next.

- ➤ Write a letter to the person you're angry with, and then decide whether to send it or tear it up.
- ➤ Let the person you're angry with know why you're angry, but do it in a calm, nonconfrontational way. Say, "I disagree with that," instead of "You are so totally wrong."
- ➤ Recognize the signs that show your anger is building, and distract yourself or do some deep, relaxing breathing.
- ➤ Take a moment to reflect on what the other person is feeling and why. Understanding the other person's perspective might just snap the anger cycle.
- ➤ Ask yourself, "Is this really worth getting angry about?"

> ❝ I need to listen to music when I'm really, really angry. I also like to vent to my friends and parents. What makes me angry with the most regularity is closed-minded people. ❞
>
> —SAMANTHA, 16

> ❝ I don't really get angry with anyone outside my family, and with my family, I just yell or whatever at the moment and get over it within, like, fifteen minutes or so. I occasionally get annoyed with friends, and then I typically just bite my tongue— not literally—and get over it. ❞
>
> —ROB, 19

LOSS AND GRIEVING TIME

Grief is very personal. There's no right or wrong way to deal with the death of someone close to you and no set timetable for the grief process. The way you grieve partly depends on the circumstances. If a grandparent or some other relative has been ill for many years and has been slowly deteriorating, death is expected, and to some degree, may even be a relief for you and your family. While you will be sad, you have gotten used to the loss of that person in your life.

My grandfather died last year. He was really old and sick, and I was really sad that he died, because he was a great person and an amazing role model. I basically dealt with the grief pretty well, because his death wasn't a complete shock.

—MEGHAN, 19

When you are faced with an unexpected loss, whether it's a friend or a grandparent, your first emotion may well be shock and disbelief. You might wake up in the morning, thinking that you were just having a nightmare. It takes a while for the reality to set in. You may question why this is happening to you. And you may get angry. That's all perfectly normal.

Death is unfair and sad and overwhelming. In time, the intense sadness usually passes, although the memories of that person stay with you. Some people your age feel guilty when they find themselves having a good time shortly after someone close to them has died. Sometimes the guilt is associated with something you said to or about the person who died, which you now feel was wrong. You don't have to punish yourself and cry all the time. A lot of grief stays inside and is part of your private moments. Your deep sense of grief does diminish in time, but many people find that weeks, months, or even years after a death, something happens that brings the sadness back almost full-blown. It could be hearing a song or seeing a person who resembles the relative or friend who died. Don't panic when that happens, since those strong feelings will subside. However, a new loss, even something like a close friend moving away, can reawaken old pain.

Here are some ways you can cope when someone close to you dies:

➤ Give yourself permission to cry. Tears offer a natural emotional release.
➤ Do something creative with your sadness (paint, write a poem or a story, compose a piece of music).
➤ Attend the funeral or memorial service. While participating might be very painful, you may be able to get a sense of closure you otherwise couldn't achieve.
➤ Talk to others who are going through the same experience. If a classmate dies, you might want to get together with other kids in your class to talk about the classmate. It's okay to share funny stories.
➤ Talk about your feelings to a parent or a guidance counselor or another caring adult, someone who is understanding and compassionate.
➤ Do something meaningful in the name of the person who has died. Donate money or time to a cause that was important to that person.

> " Last spring, a friend fell while hiking, rupturing his spleen and dying of internal bleeding. I still haven't gotten over it, but it helps that we are from a very close religious community, and we all mourn his loss together. "

—ALUSANI, 17

> " My nanny died a couple of years ago. My parents didn't even tell me until months later. When I found out, I just cried and got it out of my system. "

—WENDY, 19

“ My grandfather was always at my house—he lived five minutes away from us. He was an alcoholic on and off throughout his life. Once, while he had been drinking, he fell and broke his arm. He came to live with us while he recuperated. All the time he was in our house, he didn't drink at all. But when he left our house, the drinking started again. My mother wouldn't let him come back to our house. Finally, the day he was supposed to go to a rehab place, he got drunk and fell. He was taken to the hospital, where he had a heart attack and died. That's why I'll never drink. Even though my grandfather died a year ago, sometimes I think I hear him in the house, and then I remember that he's dead. **”**

—ISABELLA, 16

OTHER KINDS OF LOSS

If your parents have divorced, you know about loss. Even if your mom and dad have a joint custody arrangement, you don't see them as much as you did when they were together. And because of all of the things already scheduled into your life, figuring out where you need to be, when you need to get there, and which parent will be there can become a logistical nightmare for you and your parents. If one or both of your parents are pressuring you to take sides, it's hard to stay out of the direct line of fire. Remind yourself that divorce is something that parents do to each other and not to their kids.

“ My parents were officially divorced when I was 12. For some time before that, my father had lived with us, but my parents were clearly living separate lives. My sister and I kind of knew that something was off all along, so when my mom told us, we weren't surprised. It was actually kind of a relief. My sister probably felt the divorce more than me, since she was 'daddy's girl.' My dad stayed in the apartment where we had lived, and my sister, mom, and I moved out. For a while, my father was still very much involved in our lives. He would fix things around the house we moved into. But then after a while, something happened. Once we stopped needing him, he backed off. To me, that's not a valid reason for backing away from us. To this day, I'm still annoyed.

My parents only talk to each other about legal matters. I do see my dad at least once a week, but he won't even knock on the door when he comes to pick me up. Sometimes, he even parks on the corner. My dad said that he doesn't date, that he's done with that phase of his life. My mom did some casual dating for a while. Now, she's been seeing the same guy for about three years. I'm happy that she's happy, but I wish that I knew this guy more. It's still awkward around him. We've only sat down for dinner a handful of times. He doesn't know how to act around teenage girls. My mom would like to get married, but he's afraid of commitment. If they decided to get married, it would be weird for us, because we just don't know him. 99

—MARIE, 16

What about the loss of a beloved pet? Don't let anyone get away with saying: "What are you so upset about? It was only a bird [or a cat or a mouse]." When you care about an animal, its death can be very sad. That pet was part of your life, part of your family. Grieving is a normal reaction. Maybe a quiet ceremony or an opportunity to write a song or poem about the pet might help. If you have a friend who has been through a similar experience or is usually sympathetic, talk about your situation.

> A couple of years ago, my guinea pig got really sick and died. I was really sad. I buried her in my backyard in a shoebox with her name on it. It sounds a little silly now, but I felt that I needed to do that.

—DANIELLE, 16

WHEN IT'S MORE THAN SADNESS

Sadness and depression are not the same thing. People get sad for all kinds of reasons. Maybe you broke up with a boyfriend or girlfriend. Perhaps you didn't make the varsity sports team that was so important to you. Or maybe you failed a test in a subject you usually do well in. Feeling down from these kinds of events happens to everyone—it's hard to make it through high school without some sadness.

If you're feeling down, talk to someone about what you're going through. You don't want to hear them tell you that you shouldn't feel sad. What help is that? But you probably do want someone to listen to you without trying to fix the problem. And if you do want some suggestions for solving a problem, be sure to ask for that.

> Sometimes, I stay in bad moods for a long time. I can start feeling sad about something that happened on Monday, and on Friday I'm still thinking about the same thing.

—ANNE, 16

Clinical depression—that's the official name—is more extreme and longer-lasting than ordinary sadness. About one in twelve teens suffers from this kind of serious depression before the age of 18, with girls about twice as likely as boys to show signs. Your friends might notice your depression before you do, and you might notice it before your parents do. If you're really depressed, you might sleep much more than you usually do, or have the opposite problem, waking up very early and not being able to get back to sleep or tossing and turning all night long. You might eat much more than is typical for you, as if stuffing yourself can ease your pain. Or you might have almost no interest in food. In fact, one of the key symptoms of depression is a loss of interest in those things that used to give you pleasure, like being with friends, doing well in school, listening to music. You just don't have the energy to do much of anything.

If you're experiencing any of these symptoms, it's important to get checked out by a doctor. Physical illnesses can cause some of these same symptoms. But if the problem isn't physical, you might be suffering from clinical depression. Sometimes depression occurs after an unbearable loss (like that of a parent), but sometimes there's nothing in particular that sets off the depression. Talk to a parent or a doctor right away, particularly if your symptoms are intense or have already lasted a few weeks, so you can get the professional help that you need.

66 My older sister was hospitalized with depression when she was a junior in high school and I was in third grade. It was at that point that I began to feel depressed on a very mild level. In eighth grade, my depression became unbearable. One day at lunch, I just broke down in the middle of the cafeteria. I saw a therapist and was put on medication, which first numbed me but eventually allowed me to recover. I spent three years relatively depression-free. In the winter of tenth grade, I decided to decrease my medication, with

the assistance of my psychologist and psychiatrist, in the hopes of remedying some of the side effects.

I began the fall of my junior year with a lot of hope—I was secretary of Junior Statesmen of America, planning to start a peace club, and I was taking AP American history, Spanish 3 Honors, and Scholars English. For a while, everything was okay, but it became clear that I was not. My therapist asked me if I thought I was depressed again, and that opened Pandora's box. No, I thought, that's over, I'm fine. But then I realized I was not. My medication was increased, and then I was switched to something new. Then I was introduced to a new phenomenon: anxiety. Depression slows you down, makes everything the same low, wet-towel feeling, but anxiety makes your mind race and your pulse go faster. The world spins around you, and there's no way to stop it.

I didn't want to be alive, but I never wanted to die. In February, I was hospitalized for the worst week of my life, trying to explain to everyone there that a sterile environment full of sick kids and completely devoid of love was not what I needed to heal. So where am I now? I'm about to start an intensive day treatment program to make up all the schoolwork I've missed. I'm on two medications, and I still suffer from depression and anxiety. But the main thing for me now is to get over the things I've lost: the clubs, the honors classes, my confidence. I am determined to graduate with the rest of my class, and I no longer want to give up. 99

—HELEN, 17

Audrey Jacobs Brockner is a licensed clinical social worker. Here's what she has to say about therapy.

Many teens—and adults, too, for that matter—wonder if going to talk to a psychotherapist is a sign of "weakness." It's anything but that. It takes personal strength to let someone be a guide. Psychotherapy is a partnership. The therapist's job is to join with you to help figure out what and how internal demons are interfering in your life. With a therapist, you decide the course of treatment. Therapy just helps you get your life journey back on track and able to feel more joy. Adolescence is like driving in a new territory; having a driver and a navigator always makes the trip easier. The bottom line is that talking to someone, while difficult at first, can be very helpful.

CUTTING

Some high school kids who have trouble expressing their intense feelings in other ways cut themselves, or else injure themselves through some other means (burning themselves or hitting themselves with an object hard enough to cause bruising, for example). People who cut themselves usually say they do it to relieve tension, which may work for them, but only for a short time. That's why cutting can become addictive. It feels good for the moment and provides a temporary sense of control, a way to eliminate deep emotional pain. But the tension eventually rises again, and the need to cut becomes overwhelming. Although cutting is more common among girls, guys, too, engage in this behavior. Typically, cutters don't want to injure themselves permanently, but cutting comes with a variety of risks. The cut might be deeper than intended, the cutting object (maybe scissors or a razor blade) is not sterile and the cut can become infected, or the cutting object might spread disease, such as hepatitis, when two people share the same instrument.

People who self-injure usually try to hide what they're doing from their friends and family. If you recognize that a friend is a cutter, don't ignore it. Talk about what you've seen, reminding the person that you care and want to help. Encourage your friend to talk to a parent or a counselor to get help. If your friend doesn't want to talk directly to a parent or a professional, suggest that he or she write a letter to that person, describing what's going on. If you've been injuring yourself, get help in stopping the cycle—the sooner, the better. Treatment might include medication, stress reduction activities, or therapy for an underlying problem such as depression or an eating disorder.

> When my sister started college last year, she hardly ever went to class. My mom and I were really angry with her. We were cutting back on everything at home so she could go to college, and my sister just wouldn't acknowledge that my mom was making this sacrifice for her. My mom thought that my sister was being lazy, and I thought the same thing. But there began to be other signs that something was wrong—she was sad a lot of the time, she didn't have friends to hang out with. Finally, my mom got my sister to see a therapist, and we all found out that my sister had been cutting herself. She was doing it because she was depressed. It took me a long time to recognize that she had a real problem. I had thought that my sister was faking her problems. But when I realized that she was cutting herself, I knew that her problems were real, and I felt terrible that I had not understood what she was going through.

—ILANA, 15

Stepping in to Help Your Friends

You may be in a position not only to notice when your friends are having serious problems before their parents do but also to have more of an influence on your friends than they do. With a lot of situations involving friends, you'll be able to help them deal with their problems directly. Maybe your friend is disappointed about a bad grade in chemistry, but she seems like her regular self, nothing out of the ordinary. You talk for a while, and she regains her perspective and realizes it's only one test, not the end of the world. You're back to discussing party plans for the weekend.

> I can tell when people are upset. They react differently to me. Someone who's usually outgoing goes off to sit in a corner, and the person who usually stays in a corner suddenly starts acting real friendly. That's a sure sign that's something's wrong.
>
> —SAM, 16

> I know when my friends are having emotional problems either because they talk to me about them or because I realize that they're not as excited or enthusiastic as normal, or they're different in some other way that makes it seem as though something is wrong.
>
> —ROB, 19

> **"** When my friends are upset, the volume level or the pitch of their voice gets higher. Crying, too, is a dead giveaway. **"**

—RACHEL, 17

You should know when it's time to call in the big guns—a parent or a guidance counselor or a school psychologist. For instance, suppose your friend is seriously depressed and has been saying that his family would be better off without him or something like that, but he then asks you not to tell anyone what he's just told you. You're in a tough spot. This is the situation where you immediately need to get some adult help—your mom or dad, his parents, a teacher, a school nurse, someone who's going to take action. Although you might think you would be betraying a friend by talking to an adult after you've been asked to keep something confidential, you're actually a much better friend when you get help from an adult in these situations. You might be saving your friend's life. What about when you're not sure? Have you heard the expression "Better safe than sorry"? Here's the time to use it. When you're not certain about what to do, err on the side of telling.

Here is a hotline number you should know when you or your friends are in serious emotional trouble: 1-800-SUICIDE (1-800-784-2433). You can also get help online by logging on to safeyouth.org. In an emergency, call 911 to get immediate help.

> **"** My friends are pretty open about their problems. Usually they'll talk to me. The one friend who sometimes doesn't will get very quiet and try to isolate herself. I always try to get her to talk to me, and she usually does. I only talk about her problems to my parents if they've gotten bad enough that she's contemplating suicide. **"**

—SAMANTHA, 16

Michael A. Tedesco is a high school guidance counselor. Here is what he has to say about helping a friend in need.

If your friend is dealing with a serious problem, don't hesitate to talk to your guidance counselor. When you intercede to help someone, you may need to take a risk, find the courage to follow through, and put yourself on the line. Your counselor can help you figure out how to best help your friend. You may be the one connection this friend has. When students come to me about a friend, I try to get the student with the problem to talk to me. I may need to involve the school psychologist and school nurse, even the parents, if the student says that I can do that. What's important is getting sensitive, caring help to students who need it.

> " I have a friend who is an insomniac. She never sleeps. One of my other friends talked to her guidance counselor about this girl. When the insomniac found out, she felt betrayed. The counselor couldn't really do anything but tell the friend what to do. I guess it wasn't a big enough problem to call her parents or anything. "
>
> —ISABELLA, 16

Stressed Out?

Not surprisingly, school is probably the biggest stressor in your life. Friends who treat you badly, relationships gone sour, and problems in a family are other sources of stress. You may also be worried about war and terrorism. In a 2005 Gallup Youth Survey, almost a third of 13- to 17-year-olds said they were somewhat or very worried about someone in their family being the victim of a terrorist attack.

COPING WITH STRESS

Running away from your problems will only make you more anxious, while facing up to them can build your self-confidence. Since stress in life is inescapable, you might as well develop some good techniques for coping with it. Setting priorities and managing your time better are two ways to cope with the stress that comes from being overwhelmed with schoolwork and other responsibilities. Find out more about those topics in Chapter 6.

Teens around the country shared what stresses them and how they cope with those feelings. Take a clue from one of them, or create your own stress management strategy. The important thing is to find a way to reduce some of the tension you're dealing with and to remember the most effective techniques when your stress starts going off the scale.

> All of my friends are constantly talking about how much they have to do, and by the time they're finished talking about this stuff, I'm as stressed as they are. I write down everything that I have to do, and then I tear up the paper into little bits. Sometimes I don't even bother to write anything on the paper—I just tear it up to get rid of my stress. Brown paper bags are good for this. Sometimes having a cup of tea helps, too.

—LIAN, 16

" Sometimes I get really stressed when one of my friends—a very troubled girl—has to vent to me. I'm glad she does, but it leaves me very tense and drained. Listening to music is a good solution to that kind of stress. **"**

—SAMANTHA, 16

" Eating ice cream and sleeping usually help reduce my stress. Otherwise, I do stupid things like throw my phone or other objects across the room or punch the walls. **"**

—AALIYAH, 16

" I write in my online journal because there are things I want to get out, things that I don't feel completely comfortable talking to others about. When I write, it provides a sort of catharsis for me. A lot of the time, I just think about things in my head, and I'll end up going in circles, not really going anywhere. But when I write it all down, it's usually clearer, since I have to think each thing out before I can put it into words. It's also nice when people respond to what I've written, because then I know that they care about what's going on in my life. **"**

—KEITH, 19

> **"** My dog makes me feel better because I can tell her what's going on—problems at school or with my mom. My dog licks my face, and I know everything will be okay. **"**

—CHARLOTTE, 16

> **"** When people really bother me, I call them names in my head, not to their face, which helps a little. **"**

—LAKSHMAN, 16

> **"** If I'm in a really bad mood, I'll usually run or play tennis, because you can get out your aggression through exercise rather than sitting there feeling sorry for yourself. **"**

—ELIZABETH, 16

Jot down a few stress-busting ideas. Since writing stuff down helps people remember, hopefully one of these ideas will come to you during a major stress attack.

COLLEGE APPLICATION ANGST

One of the most stressful times of the high school years is during the college search and application process. Applying to college is more than writing some essays and filling out application forms. It's a personal investment with emotional fallout. Students in their first year of high school are already worried about getting into college, particularly about finding the "right" college. In fact, many kids started worrying in elementary school, something that didn't happen years ago. No wonder you're freaking out.

❝ I don't do anything now just to learn or to have fun. I just do everything because it will look good on my college application. I have no stress management skills. I just procrastinate—it's instant gratification, but then I still have to get the work done. Talking to my friends doesn't help, because they have the same problems that I do. **❞**

—EILEEN, 16

❝ I have had college burned into my mind since first grade. If you ask my mom, she'll deny it, but it's true. My brother goes to Harvard, and I have no chance of going anywhere like that. **❞**

—REBECCA, 16

College students have lots of advice for high school students about dealing with the emotional issues surrounding the college application process. They've been through the drama, so they're worth listening to.

❝ Don't worry too much about getting into a particular school. It's not really the end of the world if you don't get into Harvard or Yale or whatever you have your heart set on. Most students will be happy wherever they end up going. **❞**

—ROB, 19

66 Don't get too stressed about getting in. Once you've filed your application, you just have to wait it out and figure out where you'll fit in. 99

—MOLLY, 19

66 I didn't get into my first-choice school, so I ended up going somewhere else, which definitely worked out for the best. Now I can't imagine myself anywhere but where I am. 99

—MEGHAN, 19

66 Remember to pick a decent safety school. Once you get in there, you'll be able to breathe again, because you know you're going to college. 99

—TIM, 20

You can read more about college applications in Chapter 6. Because applying to college and dealing with other difficult situations can become stressful, even overwhelming at times, you may need to remind yourself that life is also about laughing, hanging out, and having fun.

Parents, Privacy, and Parties

> " My parents and I fight most of the time about school. They keep telling me not to screw up. If I do mess up on my report card or progress report, I get kind of a lecture, the same one each time, so I get that lecture six times a year. "
>
> —DAVID, 15

Independence, Privacy, and Curfews: Negotiating for the Big Things

Do you sometimes feel as if you're negotiating a multi-billion-dollar contract when you try to get your parents to agree to a later curfew on Friday nights? The high school years are a time when you want more and more independence and your parents are probably getting more and more nervous about what you might do with all that independence. The high school years are typically filled with family conflict as your needs and your parents' concerns collide, sometimes very loudly. You're still surrounded by your family's love, but the relationship is now often flavored by opposing perspectives—at least some of the time.

> My friend Veronica's parents would lock her up in a plastic bubble if they could. They give her the third degree about coming over to my house, and I live across the street from her.
>
> —SHIRA, 16

> Sometimes my parents have trouble accepting that I am more independent now. They can be overprotective and clingy.
>
> —EMILY, 16

> To end a fight, I say whatever my parents want to hear. It's bending the truth, but then I don't have to sit there for another hour listening to them.
>
> —JASON, 15

Note that when the term *family* is used in this chapter, that means any possible configuration that's out there, including yours. And when parents are mentioned, that could mean mom and dad or mom alone or two moms or two dads or just dad or maybe a grandparent if that's the person who's mainly responsible for you.

YOUR GROWING INDEPENDENCE

Maybe you've always been the independent sort—you knew exactly what shirt you wanted to wear to school and did not take into account either the weather or your mom's opinion. Or perhaps you were the type who generally relied on others—friends or family—to make decisions for you. Regardless of where you started out when you hit the teen years, you're becoming more independent. That's a good thing, because soon you'll be out on your own.

The high school years are a time when you get to try out your freedom without it getting too scary. You can always go home—for advice and a little comforting. Asserting your independence while staying connected to your family is one of the important tasks of these years. Don't think it happens in one day or even one year. Be patient with yourself—and with your parents. They're learning to let go, particularly if you're the oldest in the family. And while you might have to give them a little nudge from time to time—"I'm in high school now, remember?"—don't be surprised if they remind you every once in a while that you do have a home address.

> " I just want to be able to drive. My mom won't let me take the driver's test until I've had lots more practice. Maybe that's because I sometimes have trouble figuring out my right from my left. "
>
> —CHARLOTTE, 16

> " I have always needed my own space, but when I started high school, I began to feel the influence of my parents more, like everything seemed to matter more and I couldn't be trusted to handle it on my own. It was because I felt suffocated at home that I went to spend a semester abroad. As soon as I got home, they went right back to 'mother-henning' and micromanaging my time. "
>
> —ANNE, 16

Parents, Privacy, and Parties: Find the Balance   **55**

> **My parents trust me, so I don't need to ask for more independence.**
>
> —RASHEED, 16

> **We fought a lot in high school, especially during my senior year, about how much freedom I had. I felt like they wouldn't let me do a lot of things, and they didn't always give very good reasons.**
>
> —WILL, 19

What if your parents are the type who give you so much freedom that it almost seems as if they don't care what you're doing and who you're doing it with? Most likely, they do care, but they may be so busy with their own lives—demanding jobs, money troubles, and who knows what else—that they aren't as involved as they could or should be. You may have to be more of the adult in these situations. That may not be fair, but if that's what's going on in your family, you have no choice but to deal with it. Be as direct as you can in telling them that you'd appreciate more time with them and more questions. And find supportive adults in other places—a youth leader at your house of worship, maybe a guidance counselor or a caring teacher, or an understanding aunt or uncle.

> **My dad gets home late most of the time, so he doesn't do or say much about anything.**
>
> —JAKE, 15

Private Time and Space

You have already told your parents a zillion times that they must knock before coming into your room. And you have forbidden them from reading your online journal—the info is only for your fifty closest friends, and besides, you know that your parents would take everything you've written out of context. A recent study found that half of the teenagers in the United States prefer to write in a blog rather than open up and discuss issues with a parent.

You may be asking yourself, "Why do my parents keep barging in? Why do they constantly beg to read my journal or, even worse, secretly figure out how to access it?" Because they hate that you are growing up, and they're totally scared that you're doing something that will destroy your life. No matter how levelheaded you've always been, parents are truly terrified of what you might do. That's partly because they know what they tried at your age, and they'd like you to learn from their experience. That's probably impossible, but it doesn't prevent them from trying.

Because all of us need space and alone-time for daydreaming, reading, and even goofing off, find a way to get the message across to your parents. Help them see your perspective: Would they want you to enter their bedroom when the door's closed or to open mail addressed to them? You respect their privacy; you'd like them to respect yours.

> " My parents gave me privacy, but they were also the type who liked to be involved, which, as a high school student, is not something you really want all the time. They never violated my personal space, went through my stuff, or listened to my phone conversations, but they always wanted to know where I was going. "
>
> —BERNARDO, 19

Expert Advice

Social worker Diane Tukman has run group discussion sessions with teens for twenty years. Here is what she has to say about teen privacy.

Everyone needs some amount of privacy—time alone without others barging in, demanding to know what's on your mind. What do you do when your parents don't understand your need to keep some things private? Communication is the key. The best way to get your message across is to be clear about your needs. Be honest and straightforward. Let them know that you've shut your door because you need some time alone, maybe to think through some things on your own. You're not keeping them out of your life; you're just keeping some of you inside.

66 My mom sometimes comes into my bedroom without knocking, which I mind on principle, not because I have anything to hide. 99

—LAURIE, 15

66 My mom is incredibly nosy, while my dad is uninvolved in my life. He gets a lot of his information through my mom's nosiness. 99

—KEVIN, 17

We pretty much go by a 'don't ask, don't tell' policy unless the subject is school. Then they have to know every single grade that my teachers have given me and every remark they've made.

—REBECCA, 16

Negotiating Curfews

Most kids are expected to be home immediately after their extracurricular activities on school days, so curfews during the week are typically a non-issue. Come the weekend, and the rules change. Some parents have precise curfews (without exception, you are to be home by midnight), while other parents do not set a specific curfew but just want their kids to stay in touch, usually by cell phone, as they go from place to place. Make sure you know which applies to you. A situation that you want to avoid is your dad waking up at three in the morning to find you not home when you had an agreed-on curfew of 1:00 A.M. "I didn't realize how late it was—I wasn't wearing a watch" is not an excuse that will keep you out of hot water.

Typically, curfews are a problem for high school students only when theirs is significantly earlier than friends' curfews. If you're going to negotiate for a later time, make your request reasonable. You'll have a better chance of success if the time you request is not too much later than your original curfew. And if you do get the later curfew, be sure to get home by your new time, so your parents will see you as responsible and mature. They might even agree to negotiate a later time at a future date.

Don't feel that you always have to stay out until the clock precisely strikes your curfew time. Surprise your parents, and come home earlier sometimes. Particularly once you've started driving or your friends have, they'll worry. No matter how many times you tell them they don't have to, that you're responsible and use good judgment, they'll still worry. So when you get home early, you've given them one night of no worrying. If you're lucky, they'll remember that when you negotiate for something else. And, if you're going to miss your curfew for any reason—you were having a great time at a party or the traffic was insane—call home. It's easier for parents to overlook a missed curfew when you've been considerate than to forgive you when you didn't bother to call.

A Gallup study of teens found that the most common punishment from parents for missing a curfew was being grounded or having privileges taken away—more than twice as common as yelling or lecturing. So if you'd like to keep spending time with friends, keep track of time when you're hanging out with them.

> I have a 1:00 A.M. curfew. I just call when I want to get picked up.
>
> —JOSH, 16

> In high school, my curfew was 2:00 A.M. on the weekends. Toward the end of my senior year, it was 2:30. I think the curfew was fair, but only because all of my friends had curfews.
>
> —ELIOT, 19

> I had a curfew of midnight, which I hated. It was a pain to leave places so early to get home. I understand why I had it, but I don't think the hour was appropriate. I wouldn't have minded 1:00 A.M. My parents had a midnight curfew for me because they said they didn't want me driving

late when there were drunk drivers out, and also so they could sleep more soundly, knowing I was home and alive. That didn't always sit well with me, because half the time they were already sleeping when I got home, or on, like, a Tuesday night in July, there usually weren't any drunk drivers lurking about in my small town. 99

—ALYSSA, 19

66 My parents enforced their curfew more heavily when I started driving. Before that, I didn't even really have one. Once I was driving, they let me go where I wanted as long as I was home by the curfew. 99

—ORTIZ, 19

What if your parents don't bother with curfews? Does that mean they don't care about you? Absolutely not. Maybe they know that you're the type who doesn't need one. Or they just don't believe in lots of rules for their kids. Then you may need to be more responsible and figure out what rules you want to set for yourself.

66 For the most part, my curfew is self-imposed. This is because I need an insane amount of sleep to be even functional each day. I can barely move if I get only eight hours of sleep. So, pretty much, my parents just leave me alone, and if I'm tired the next morning, it was my own fault. 99

—SAMANTHA, 16

> **❝** I don't have a curfew, but my dad will not go to bed until I am home—although he always falls asleep on the couch—so I try not to come home very late. **❞**

—ANDREW, 17

Dramas and Traumas

One of the best things about being part of a family is that you get to be totally yourself—no Oscar-winning acting is needed to be accepted and loved. But when you're in the midst of a major family drama, you may think your family is more dysfunctional than most, that your parents are more overprotective than others, or that your siblings are more annoying than anyone else's. Once you compare notes with your friends, it becomes very clear that every family has its own dramas and traumas. A 2005 Gallup Youth Survey found that more than a third of teens think their parents are stricter than most of their friends' parents.

> **❝** My parents are not that strict. I tell them stuff, but I edit it a lot. They know I'm going to do stuff, but they hope I'll be smart about it. They don't need to hear some of the stuff. **❞**

—JAKE, 15

> **❝** My mother makes me feel most stressed, and no matter what I do, it's never right or good enough. She doesn't necessarily say anything, but she makes this noise. I know what that means, that she disapproves. **❞**

—DAVITA, 16

> When I got bad grades in high school, I was on punishment until the next report card came out, which was: come straight home after school and do homework before TV.

—DENISHA, 20

You learn a lot from your family—how to love, how to argue, how to have fun, how to treat other people. What happens in your family affects, in profound ways, how you act in relationships that you have outside your family now and in the future. Think about the dynamics in your own family as you examine your friendships and romantic relationships.

> When I get angry with my parents, I act cold toward them and say mean things. Then I feel guilty. I don't apologize right away, but I do eventually.

—JULIE, 16

> Since my brother, who's now in college, was a good student, my mom sometimes forgets that I have a learning disability, and she expects me to do as well as him.

—TODD, 16

> I get along with my dad—we have the same sense of humor, which my mom doesn't get. So my dad and I bond over our sense of humor.

—DAVITA, 16

> **My mother bugs me about school every day, every minute that I'm not studying. The worst thing is she's usually right that I should be studying.**

—AARON, 15

COMMUNICATING WITH PARENTS

Have you ever heard someone say, "It's not what you say, but how you say it"? Well, that might not be totally true, because what you say does count for something, but tone of voice is often more important. That's because it's hard to pay attention to the content of the message when all you hear is a shrieking voice. If that voice happens to belong to you, then it's time to figure out how you can talk to your parents instead of screaming when you disagree about something.

> **My mom is really stubborn and hardheaded. She doesn't like to admit when she's wrong, even when I can tell that she realizes for a brief moment that she really is wrong.**

—MISSY, 17

> **Even if my mom were not my mom, I would still want to hang out with her. We can talk about almost everything.**

—EILEEN, 16

> **My parents and I don't fight very often, but when we do, it's about really stupid things. I get really bad-tempered when I'm overtired and PMSing. Usually I stomp off, don't talk for a while, and then come back to apologize.**
>
> —SAMANTHA, 16

All kids are going to fight with their parents. For some, fighting is a major part of the relationship, while for others, fighting is a rare occurrence. You already know what the big issues are in your family—probably some combination of chores, homework and grades, television and online time, condition of your room, friends, maybe drinking. Now think about *how* you fight. Is it pretty much one-sided? Your parents yell at you, and you react with passive-aggressive behavior—you say you'll do it and then conveniently forget. Or do both of you go at it full-throttle with lots of screaming, threats, and slamming doors? Can anyone even hear the other side with those kinds of fights? Another style is the silent seething. You're both so angry that there's little real communication going on. Arms wrapped tightly across the chest and a perpetual frown are body language cues that nobody's really listening anymore.

> **Anytime we have a conversation, we fight. It's kind of fun for me, but it aggravates my parents.**
>
> —DANNY, 15

> **Family relationships get shakier during the high school years. I'm freaking out, so my parents are, too.**
>
> —ANGEL, 16

> My parents are both lawyers, so you just can't win in my family.

If your fights don't seem particularly productive, try something different. Here are some rules for fair fighting:

➤ Speak and act in a respectful way, and your parents are likely to respond in the same way. Watch your body language—make sure what you say and how you act are in sync.

➤ Listen to what your parents have to say, and expect them to listen to you. If both sides really listen to each other, a compromise might be possible.

➤ When the answer is a definite no, leave it at that. Not everything is open to negotiation. But you have a right to ask questions and get explanations.

➤ Don't exaggerate. Complaining, "You always say that," when it's not true will not help you build your case.

➤ Wait for the right moment to have an important discussion. Asking for something big when your mom has just walked into the house after an awful day at work is not likely to win you any points.

> We could have a major fight, and then the next morning, everything's fine again. Or we stop arguing when we need to eat.

—DANIELLE, 16

> 66 We don't typically have arguments. We have debates about anything and everything, from why we have to baby-sit for my cousins on the weekend to what's the proper golf technique. 99
>
> —GREG, 16

> 66 What annoys me most about my parents is that they sometimes don't appreciate who I am as an individual, but rather try to mold my life toward that of my brothers or their friends' teenage children, who might be more socially and physically and academically active. I think the pressures are so much different now than when they were teens, so they think they understand how it works, but in actuality, they are relatively naive about teenage pressures and behavior. 99
>
> —XAVIER, 17

WHEN FAMILY MEMBERS ARE ILL

Because you care so much about your family, it's hard when a member is sick or has a severe disability. What's also tough to deal with is the pity, stereotyping, or ignorance that other people show toward those who are different. If you have a friend who's going through a tough family situation, the best thing you can do is care—and listen.

> The main stress in my life is my parents. My mom has been sick all of my life, so there's a lot of grief surrounding our family, which turns into guilt because there's nothing any of us can do for her. She also hoards compulsively, so our house is not exactly the ideal environment for three children to grow up in. And I have anger issues because it's so hard to blame her—it's a disease, and I know how hard she tries.

—LAUREN, 17

> My mom makes herself physically ill by stressing herself so much. She works too hard, but then she complains about it. It scares us when she makes herself ill.

—ELENA, 16

Party Time

While parties are as natural a part of the high school years as standardized tests and pimples, parties are—with any luck—a lot more fun. Get-togethers with friends are sometimes everything you had hoped for, including meeting and spending time with the guy or girl of your dreams, but at times, parties can be downright painful. There are lots of ways for parties to go astray—everything from spilling cranberry juice down your white shirt within two minutes of the party's start to hoards of uninvited guests causing a near-riot until the police show up to control it.

Before you host a party, make sure you and your parents agree on the rules. Here's a checklist to review with them:

> What time does the party start?
> What time will the party end?
> How many people are invited?
> How many people are likely to show up?
> What arrangements have been made for kids being picked up at the end of the party?
> What kind of food and drinks are you serving?
> What are the rules about smoking and drinking?
> Who's paying for the party stuff, including food and paper goods?
> In what part of the house will parents be during the party?
> Is anyone sleeping over after the party?
> Who's cleaning up after the party? And what does cleaning up look like?

" Sometimes I do feel as if my parents are always the first ones to pick up their kid, and that they don't need to be. Sometimes I don't think that my early departure from every party is fair. But once one of my friends had a fairly small at-home party for her birthday, and both she and I were completely astonished when my parents didn't come until the very end. "

—LAURA, 16

" The big rule my parents have for parties I go to is that there has to be a designated driver. And they don't want me to drink a lot, which they define as four or more beers. They know they don't really have control over what I do. The important thing is not to get caught when the cops come. "

—NICK, 16

I was one of those angelic children, and I never had 'house parties' while my parents were out. When I did have parties, one of my parents was usually around, and there weren't really rules, but more an understanding that the guests would respect our house and property. **"**

—AMIT, 19

" When my parents leave for a weekend, I do have parties without them knowing. But my friends and I don't do anything my parents wouldn't want us to do, like drinking and drugs. **"**

—PETER, 17

" The one rule my parents were most concerned about was drinking and driving. That seems to be a legitimate and fair rule to abide by, given the fact that they let me out at night. **"**

—ELIOT, 19

Staying Connected

It's true that your family might drive you crazy from time to time. Okay, so maybe it's an everyday occurrence, but you still have a strong connection to them.

FAMILY VACATIONS, HOLIDAYS, AND RITUALS

As periods of intense family togetherness, holidays and vacations allow everyone to show off their best and worst behavior. Sometimes expectations are so high, the reality can't possibly deliver. Do your family vacations resemble those wacky escapades depicted in the movies, or are they more like extended nightmares where everyone's in your face every minute? If you're lucky—and everyone works at it—a family vacation provides a relaxing escape from the everyday craziness and a time for renewal. Be sure to take photos; that way you can keep the vacation spirit alive when you're at your wit's end trying to finish your history term paper.

> " There are crazy moments on every family vacation, when everyone's getting in your space and you're so sick of these people. "
>
> —BRIANNA, 14

> " The best part of going on vacation with your family is that they act different than they do at home. We're more like friends. "
>
> —TIM, 15

> " I hate sightseeing with my family, because I have to wait until everyone's ready to move on, and I've been ready for hours to do something different. "
>
> —MIKE, 16

What's true about family vacations can also be said about holidays. They may be occasions for reconnecting or a time for tearing your hair out. If your family doesn't have holiday rituals that are meaningful to you, create new ones, and get your family involved in the celebration. Go corny, conventional, or cool—do what works for your family.

> ❝ I hate Thanksgiving—it's a meaningless parade of food. Everyone is so enveloped in the eating. It's so extreme. ❞
>
> —GREG, 16

> ❝ I like that my whole extended family gets together for Passover. It's a warm family time when you get to talk to people you haven't seen in a long time. ❞
>
> —CHARLOTTE, 16

> ❝ My parents always insist that we go to cut down our Christmas tree as a family, which is usually fun and interesting. ❞
>
> —MEGHAN, 19

While rituals around holiday time are fairly common, many families don't like waiting for that once-a-year occasion to celebrate their relationships. Besides, everyday rituals strengthen family bonds. If your family already has special rituals, honor them by showing up and not rolling your eyes. And if they don't, why not start something new—maybe a once-a-month movie or game marathon?

One of the simplest ways to stay connected with your family is sharing dinner together. Think of these meals this way: your parents are probably a lot more interested in your life than you are in theirs, so you can be the focus of most of the conversation.

When I was in high school, we used to have Sunday night dinner together, which was nice most of the time. However, sometimes I would have liked to have gone out with my friends, especially senior year, but I felt an obligation to be at home because of how much the Sunday night dinners meant to my parents. **99**

—ELIOT, 19

SIBLING TIES

Important as friends are, they come and go in your life, but siblings are forever. Yes, your younger ones can be annoying, and your older ones can tease you mercilessly. But you share a life history, people who truly understand what it's like to grow up under that roof. Studies show that even when you don't like your sister or brother, when a crisis occurs, they're still the ones you can count on.

My 11-year-old sister is an annoyance. She's loud and obnoxious. She enjoys fighting with me and can be really aggressive. One time, she stood on the bed and just jumped on me.

—CHIYO, 16

My sister and I are best friends. Yes, she does things that infuriate me all the time, but it's good to have someone who's been through all that family stuff with me. My friends don't know everything about my twisted family, but she does.

—ELENA, 16

" The good part of having an older brother is that he's already gone through stuff. I'll call him and tell him about stuff. He advises me. I trust him with stuff that I would never tell my parents. **"**

—JOSH, 16

" My younger brother and I are extremely close, but I wish I had a better relationship with my older brother—our interests are so different. As the middle child in the family, I feel like I am often blamed for nearly anything that goes wrong. **"**

—ANTONIO, 17

" It's really hard to think of something I like about my 14-year-old brother. I find him to be one of those people who don't even have to be in the same room to be annoying and someone who I would *never* associate with if I had a choice. He is only tolerable in small doses. My 19-year-old brother and I have a better relationship. Although he can be a real stuck-up chauvinist know-it-all, a lot of the time we relate to each other and therefore talk about random, meaningless things. At least we willingly talk to each other. **"**

—SHOQUANNA, 17

I see my younger siblings—my 17-year-old sister and 12-year-old brother—doing things that would have been a huge thing when I first wanted to do them. My parents were more overprotective toward me because I was the oldest. But I did like the fact that I was the first to do stuff. I also like being looked up to as a role model by my younger siblings.

—MEGHAN, 19

The one thing that most agree on when it comes to siblings: they hate being compared with each other. Parents sometimes do that without even realizing it.

I'm held up to an impossible standard—my older brother who goes to an Ivy League college—even though my parents don't think they're doing that.

—KIM, 15

When you have an older sibling, sometimes you feel like you're in their shadow. They may be really good at something. My sister, on the other hand, is a screw-up, so I feel like I have to be really good at everything to make up for that. I'm expected to learn from her mistakes.

—GRAZIA, 16

BEING AN ONLY CHILD

If you're an only child in your family, you might have a cousin or a really close friend you fight with but also love. Often those ties are as strong as the ones between siblings. Many kids who don't have siblings see advantages in their status: namely, you don't have to share your parents with another kid, and you don't have to deal with daily teasing or constant comparisons.

> 66 I think the best thing about not having siblings is not being expected to be their caretaker, as happens to one of my friends. She frequently gives up her free time because she has to care for them. 99

—RANDY, 16

Preparing to Leave Home

If you're planning to go away to college or to get a job and live on your own after high school, separation from your parents will probably look better and better as it gets closer to the time for you to leave home. It's not unusual for tensions between parents and kids to really blossom in the senior year of high school. Isn't it easier to leave someone you've been fighting with than someone you've been getting along with? But you may also feel a little apprehensive about what's ahead when your usual safety net is no longer close at hand.

You and your parents can both start preparing for the physical and emotional separation long before it happens. See Chapter 8 for tips on managing your life that will help you in your life post-parents as well. Start by listing in the following chart all the skills and tasks you take for granted at home, things like laundry or banking or sewing that maybe someone else does for you now. And if you're already doing some or all of that stuff, you have less to learn.

Household Tasks I Need to Learn

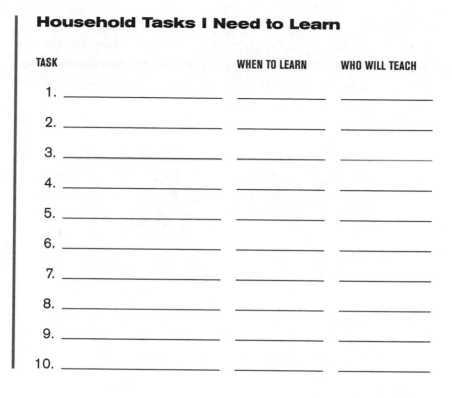

TASK	WHEN TO LEARN	WHO WILL TEACH
1. _____	_____	_____
2. _____	_____	_____
3. _____	_____	_____
4. _____	_____	_____
5. _____	_____	_____
6. _____	_____	_____
7. _____	_____	_____
8. _____	_____	_____
9. _____	_____	_____
10. _____	_____	_____

Look at that list, and make a schedule for yourself about when you're going to learn these skills and who's going to teach them. Remember that laundry only seems really simple when someone else is sorting, setting water temperatures, measuring laundry detergent, and folding clothing.

Much more difficult to deal with for you and your parents are the emotional aspects of separation. If you're the oldest child in your family, your parents need to figure out how to let go, and you're the one they're going to practice on. Sound like fun? Don't think you'll escape if you're the youngest, since they're going to be childless for the first time in many years, and that's not easy. So have a little sympathy for what they're going through, and don't say things like "I can't wait to be on my own" or "It will be so great to be out of this house" too often, even if you think them.

You might also have to prepare yourself for having a better relationship with your parents after you leave home than while you're still in high school. That's what a lot of college students say—that it's easier to have conversations and to appreciate parents from afar than when they're in your face every day.

> 66 I decide what to do and have way more freedom now that I'm in college. And I'm closer to my mom than before. I can always talk to her now about what's bothering me. 99
>
> —WINT, 19

> 66 Even though it may seem ridiculous now, you might find yourself missing home more than you thought you would when you leave. 99
>
> —ELIOT, 19

WHAT'S NEXT?

Issues that would have started World War III often get overlooked when you're not living under the same roof. While you're waiting for that time, here's some advice from college students who were in your shoes not too long ago.

> 66 Try to get along with your parents and siblings. If you already do, realize how lucky you are. When you are angry with them, try to put yourself in their shoes. I've found this to be an effective technique for resolving conflict. 99
>
> —ELIOT, 19

I think you should understand that while you might be annoyed with your parents, it is a good idea to take a moment to think about why your parents are making you or not allowing you to do something, and then try to talk to them intelligently and maturely about how you understand their thoughts. However, it is also a good idea to tell your parents where you are coming from, so that they can understand you better. Also, remember that you will be out of the house soon and will have a lot more freedom in the years to come, so just try to wait it out until that happens, if nothing else works!

—KIMBERLY, 19

The Friendship Game

> **I sat at a table with a teacher for six months. Finally, I brought popcorn because I knew I would be invited to sit at a table if I had popcorn!**
>
> —AMIE, 17

If you are new to your town or you have discovered that your closest friends have a lunch period different from yours, finding a group of friends to sit with can be a big dilemma for a lot of kids. If you are confident enough to just plop down wherever and feel the group is happy to have you at their table, go for it! But, if you are feeling a little shy as you approach that noisy room where everyone seems to be having a great time with their own group of friends, take a look at the advice from these three teens.

> **A friendship doesn't mean one plus one equals one.**
>
> —KELSEY, 16

I've found that there is nothing wrong about approaching someone you don't really know but maybe sat near in class and introducing yourself at lunch. It may seem cliché, but everyone in the beginning of the year is in the same predicament as you, and most of the time, everyone is really open to meeting new people.

I usually sat at two different tables during lunch, because I had more than one group of friends. I would table-hop from one group of friends to the next during lunch. I don't know who came up with that rule that you were only allowed to sit at one table with one crowd of kids.

—WHITNEY, 19

Look for a group that seems open and friendly. Make eye contact. If someone smiles, take a seat. If you meet kids in class or at orientation, try to find someone who has the same lunch period as you, and make plans to meet. Also look for kids who are in other groups you belong to: church, sports, band, scouts. Soon lunch becomes the part of the day you look forward to—time to hang out and relax.

—JULIA, 14

Finding Your Seat at the Friendship Table

Finding a spot in the lunchroom is a good analogy for finding your place within a group of friends—a spot where you are comfortable enough to be yourself. The older you get, the more complicated relationships can become. What worked in third grade—you watch my back when the class bully is around, and I'll share the cookies my mom puts in my lunch—no longer makes it in high school. A friendship that no longer feels right is common. Maybe you're carrying 90 percent of the friendship, while your friend is giving a measly 10 percent. You discover new interests and new opportunities—maybe a role in the school show with rehearsals every day after school for weeks or perhaps a move up to the varsity team. As your world widens or even just changes, your friendships may need some adjusting, too. You may find yourself in the tough situation of having to quit a friendship that is stopping you from growing or moving ahead. This chapter is your guide to negotiating the friendship mazes of the high school years.

CAN BOY PLUS GIRL EQUAL FRIENDSHIP?

What do you think? Can guys and girls be just friends, or will there always be some sexual tension to make the friendship difficult? Having a member of the opposite sex in a "friends-only" relationship can be the best of both worlds. You have an "in" to how they think: "Why do guys laugh at the stupidest jokes?" "Why do girls spend hours doing nothing but talking and think that's fun?" Sometimes that kind of friendship can be hard to maintain. If one of you starts to fall for the other, watch out—the friendship might be over if your friend doesn't feel the same way. So can it happen? Yes, but you have to be really honest with each other and what you each expect the other to be.

GL's Friendship Hits and Misses

Kelly White is the executive editor of GL (formerly Girls' Life) magazine. Here's her advice for keeping friends.

Unfortunately, things don't always run smoothly on Planet Friendship, so we're here to help navigate you through the bumpy spots. If a friend is down with treating you golden, that's what we call a hit. But if she's missing the point of what friendship is all about? Keep readin' . . .

HIT: She's forever reliable when the going gets rough.
MISS: She pulls a disappearing act every time you really need her.

She's what's referred to as a fair-weather friend. She's around for all the fun times, but when you become someone in need—poof!—she's nowhere to be found. Before you chalk her off as nothing more than just a hang buddy, realize that some girls don't know how to deal in uncomfortable situations. Simply let her know that you don't expect her to fix your problems—you only need someone who will listen and maybe offer a tissue, nothing more.

HIT: She never spills your secrets.
MISS: She blabs just about everything you've ever confided to her.

Some people have a very hard time keeping juicy tidbits under wraps. If you have a pal who's a gossipy gal, be discriminating when it comes to chat sessions with her. You can still spend time having fun and sharing nonconfidential conversation, but save the super-secret stuff for someone else—or even just your journal.

HIT: She shows you basic respect.
MISS: She speaks down to you, especially when others are around.

She probably does this to make herself feel superior—but it's at your expense, and you need to tell her that. Rather than coming off in an accusing manner, explain to her how it makes you feel when she rags on you in front of the crew. Chances are, she doesn't even realize it upsets you.

HIT: She's your cheerleading squad.
MISS: She acts jealous when good things happen to you.

Jealousy is a very human reaction. That said, part of maturing is learning to show self-control when exhibiting emotions. It's perfectly normal for her to feel envious, but at the same time, she should genuinely be happy for you if you make the school play or pep squad or lacrosse team or whatever. If her behavior is outwardly mean-spirited and raining on your parade, it's time for a chitchat. Tell her straight up, "Best friends need to be supportive of each other, not bring each other down."

HIT: She always has your back.
MISS: She suddenly loses her will to speak whenever you could use someone to stick up for you.

Assertiveness truly is an acquired skill, so don't fault her if she hasn't mastered it just yet. But if she's standing there and pretending she doesn't know you while you're being picked on by your school's plastic-posse, something is seriously wrong. At the very least, she should be right by your side and letting her pal-presence be known. At best, she'll learn to speak up when the meanies are doing their intimidation thing—and, of course, you'll do the same for her. Right?

66 Girls have a completely different perspective from guys, and that's one of the advantages for me of having girls as friends. They help me get inside a woman's head. When they have PMS, that's a problem sometimes, but I've learned how to deal with it. The one thing I had to learn, since I'm a touchy-feely kind of guy, is that a girl might think I'm trying to hit on her when I'm really not. The girls who've known me forever understand that it's about friendship, not anything sexual. 99

—JOE, 15

66 In high school, my best friend of the opposite sex was Ying, a girl next door. I would often go over to her house when I was free and just stay over for long periods of time, just talking and laughing about stuff. The best thing about a nonromantic relationship with a person of the opposite sex is that there are fewer complications, fewer ways that the relationship can go wrong. I think Ying and I simply expected that we'd be there for the other, to listen to what the other person had to say, and to just keep each other company. In a romantic relationship, there are many more factors—physical and emotional—so it can go awry much more easily. 99

—LIANG, 19

66 Mike is the best friend I can ask for. He is awesome, and I can count on him, no matter what. I love him to death. Without him, I don't

know what I'd do. He's my best friend, and he means the world to me because he never lets me down and he's always there for me. 🙶

—AMANDA, 15

Friendship Hits and Misses Checklist

Use this checklist to see if each of your friendships is a hit or a miss.

	YES	NO	SOMETIMES
1. My friend supports me 24/7.	_____	_____	_____
2. I can tell my friend anything and know my friend will be cool.	_____	_____	_____
3. I trust my friend to give me good advice.	_____	_____	_____
4. My friend would never betray me.	_____	_____	_____
5. My friend gives me space when I need it.	_____	_____	_____
6. My friend listens and understands what I'm really saying.	_____	_____	_____
7. My friend is loyal even in tough situations.	_____	_____	_____
8. Our friendship is 50/50.	_____	_____	_____
9. My friend pays attention and remembers what's most important to me.	_____	_____	_____
10. My friend and I have fun when we're together.	_____	_____	_____

SCORING: It's okay if you answered "sometimes" to a few statements, but even one "no" should start warning bells going off in your head. Do you really want to be stuck in a friendship with someone who not only can't remember that you have a travel soccer game every Saturday afternoon in the spring but also doesn't even begin to understand why you're really not available for anything else? And what about being friends with someone who drops you at the slightest hint of an invite to a cool party? Friends who treat you like you're not worth much—are you willing to settle for that?

> " I had a friend who thought popularity was more important than the people she had been friends with forever. When I confronted her about her sudden change of mind, she got really mad and yelled at me. Our friendship ended then. She has a new set of friends, and so do I. "
>
> —NANCY, 15

IF . . . THEN

When you make a new friend, you almost have a honeymoon period—it's a lot like falling in love. You show your best sides to each other. You put up with things that may be annoying, but you don't want to jeopardize the friendship. You make plans to do lots of fun things together. But, when the "honeymoon" is over, you start to take your friendship for granted. Your schedules conflict. You get busy. Life happens. Maybe you . . .

➤ Move
➤ Switch schools
➤ Get a job
➤ Start your college search

➤ Get really involved with someone
➤ Head in a different direction
➤ Find a new group to hang with

Some of these situations are survivable. If you and your friend have a rubber-bandy type of relationship—you each go and do your thing but snap back before the friendship that ties you can break, you're okay.

If you move—hey, that's why e-mail was invented. And maybe you can convince your parents to use up some frequent-flier miles for some face time with the friend you left behind.

If you switch schools—lucky you to have a friend who is out of the daily school drama but can listen and advise you with no agenda. And your friend can keep you up on the latest school gossip.

If you get a job—then try to match up lunch or dinner breaks to spend together. What about a morning jog before work on Saturday or a midnight snack at the diner?

If you start your college search—and you're probably heading to different coasts—plan how your college breaks can be maxed to your advantage, and make sure your cell has unlimited long distance coast-to-coast.

If you get really involved with someone—know that yes, you may spend every waking moment and your dream time involved in the love of your life, but also know that having a friend to back you up if your dream date turns out to be a nightmare disaster is critical to bouncing back. And spending time away from your cutie just makes you appreciate the relationship all the more. Plus, who but your best friend will listen for the thousandth time to the full story of how you two met?

If you head in a different direction—think about taking your friend with you. Maybe not going the whole distance, but if your sports star is soaring, having a friend as your biggest cheerleader—and there for you if an injury sidelines you for a game or two—can bring you closer. If you like chess and your friend likes lacrosse, no big deal. Friends don't have to share the same interests, just the same values, like loyalty, honesty, and trust.

If you find a new group to hang with—think about what the new group is offering you that you find really appealing, and what your old friendship isn't. If your friend is worth keeping, you could make him or her part of the group or save part of your friendship time for your old friend. But if you have really thought about it and know you have moved to a very different place and your friend won't or can't follow, it may be time to say good-bye, game over.

What Kids Have to Say About Moving On

"Jessica and I became friends when we were 3 years old. We spent a lot of time together for a long time. Sometimes I wanted to spend time with other friends, but she'd just invite herself over. Jessica was always ordering me around. A couple of years ago, we were sitting outside talking, when she asked me to get her a glass of water, and I quickly ran inside to get it for her. I think that's when it hit me—I was sick of taking orders from her. Since we're neighbors, I still see Jessica all the time, but we're no longer friends."

—RAYNA, 17

"Beth and I met at camp in the summer before third grade. When we found out we were in the same class, we were both so excited. We were best friends for years. Suddenly, in our first year of high school, Beth started being mean to me— whispering, passing notes about me. I hated it, but I still tried to keep the friendship alive and even apologized to her when I knew I hadn't done

When Friendships End

Dr. Cheryl Dellasega is the author of Girl Wars *and* Mean Girls Grow Up *and the founder of Club Ophelia. Here is what she has to say about fixing friendships.*

Friendships seem to end in two different ways. Sometimes a fight leads to lots of hurt and misunderstanding. The people involved hear only the angry words and feel confused, rejected, and embarrassed. In Club Ophelia, one girl set a goal to patch up a friendship that had ended with an argument. When she talked with her former friend, she was astonished to hear her friend say she had given up because she thought the first girl didn't care about their friendship. By saying "I miss you," these two girls regained a valuable relationship.

The other way friendships end is by people outgrowing each other. There's nothing really wrong. One girl (or boy) develops interests that don't include the other. If you are the one "left behind," you should move on, too, and find new friends who are a better match. If you are the one moving on, do it kindly. You could say, "I know we were really good friends, but I love spending time in band, and you don't. I spend so much time with my band friends, and I've started to feel really close to them."

The teens who do best in high school, I've found, are those who have a really wide assortment of friends. They take care of their friendships, too, just like you'd care for your car or other favorite possession.

---

anything wrong. Eventually, I made new friends, and Beth and I grew apart. Every day, I see Beth on my way to Spanish class, but we don't even say hello. **"**

—LIZ, 16

> In twelfth grade there's a lot of 'girl drama.' It's separation anxiety, because it's easier to say good-bye to people when you're angry. You're thinking about going off to college and you're a little afraid.

—AMIE, 17

> Troy and I were in kindergarten together, and that's when our friendship began. We were really tight for a long time, but then he started hanging out with kids at school I didn't like, and they didn't like me either. Troy became arrogant just like some of the jerks he became friends with. I still talk to Troy when I see him outside of school, but basically we both knew our friendship wasn't working for us any longer.

—DANNY, 15

FIVE BEST HOW-TOS FOR SURVIVING THE END OF A FRIENDSHIP

The death of a close friendship can feel tragic. The person who knew you best, your secret sharer and supporter, is gone. How do you deal with it?

> **Stay busy.** Don't take to your bed. You may be sad, but keep moving and doing. Maybe try something new that you didn't have time for before.
> **Pretend to be happy.** Even if your inside feels like a puddle of tears, keep your head up and a smile on your face. You'll eventually fool yourself into feeling better—and then really will.

> **Talk to someone**—even, heaven forbid, your parents or another adult you are close to. An older sib might work, too. Everyone's been through this. They may have some good advice. And having someone sympathetic to hear you out will make you feel much better. If you're the type, write about your feelings in a journal. Moving your sadness out of you and onto paper may help you get over it that much faster.

> **Keep your perspective.** Was your friendship really as great as you now imagine it, or does it just look that good because it's gone? It might help to focus on some aspects of the relationship that aggravated you to death.

> **Meet new people.** Join a youth group at your church or synagogue or a club at school. Look for volunteer opportunities in your community. Not only will you do some good, but you'll meet other people who share your interests.

Your Friend Has a Problem

What if you hate what your friend is doing? Okay, your friend—the sweet, silly kind of plain and conservative friend you have relied on to be steady and calm through all your choppy seas—is into some very serious stuff, very bad serious stuff. Stuff like drugs, heavy drinking, crime, a really bad crowd, or other stuff that you no way want to even be near. And you definitely don't want your friend involved with those things, either. What do you do?

Marla Paul, author of *The Friendship Crisis*, offers this advice in her book: "Listening well is a skill. That's because the overriding instinct is to try to fix our friends' problems—or interrupt and badger them with ours."

> " I had a friend who was having a hard time with school and her parents. She wanted to talk, and I became her outlet. Simply listening was more important than doing anything. She eventually worked everything out. I learned the best help I could be was just being there. "

—MADELEINE, 14

> " One kid I know was drinking a lot after school, but I didn't do anything, because he's not really a good friend. I would only do something for a close friend. Then I'd confront him and maybe talk to the guidance counselor at my school. I'd never talk to my mom—she would just overreact. "

—KEVIN, 15

Don't Give Up

Good friends don't just give up on their friends. They try to help as much as they can. Drinking and getting high, for example, can have consequences that your friend may not even see. You can help point out some of them, such as losing a driver's license, getting kicked out of school, losing a sports scholarship or a chance to go to college, even getting busted and going to jail or a detention center. Sound too dramatic? Read the papers. Lots of "good kids" have gotten caught up in stuff that has wrecked their lives. For more on this, see pages 194–95 in Chapter 9.

How do you know if your friend is dependent on drugs or alcohol? Ask yourself these questions:

- Does your friend drink or get high alone?
- Does your friend drink or get high regularly?
- Does your friend drink or get high before, during, or after school?
- Has your friend ever blacked out when high or drinking?
- Does your friend feel as if he or she can't have a good time unless drunk or high?
- Has your friend tried to quit and can't?
- Does your friend need to drink or use greater amounts of drugs to get the same high?

If you can say yes to even one question, then there is a good chance your friend has a problem. Okay, so what's next? Here are some actions you can take:

- Find a private spot and time to talk.
- Don't be dramatic and negative. Help your friend focus on her or his positive qualities.
- Be armed with some facts about drinking and drugs. A good website to check out is freevibe.com.
- Tell your friend how much you care and that's why you want to talk about drinking or getting high.
- If your friend gets angry, let her or him know you'll keep offering your support anyway and won't give up.

If you suspect that your friend's problem might be life-threatening (maybe your friend made a comment about "not wanting to live like this any longer") or a danger to others (perhaps a threat to bring a weapon to school) or just seems way too much for you to handle, get an adult involved: your parent, your friend's parent, a teacher, the school counselor or nurse, or a member of the clergy. And do it right away. No matter how mature you are, really serious problems are best handled by adults. You are not betraying your friend when you talk to an adult—getting help is the best gift of friendship you can give.

That Bully Business

" Kids used to bully me at my old high school. I didn't do anything, but I should have. I wish I could go back and tell somebody. "

—NANCY, 15

" Kids look at me and say, 'Band is geeky.' I don't care, because I know if I practice, music can take me far. "

—BONNIE, 14

" Girls can be sneaky. They are more into 'drama' and secrets. "

—MICHELE, 13

" At my high school, the bullies are usually the athletes who think everyone should look up to them. They pick on the scrawny kids or the big kids who they know won't fight back. I'm over six feet tall, and this short kid started dissing me once, and when I didn't react, he boasted to his friends, 'I just dissed that kid, and he didn't do s—— about it.' I don't want to get into fights, so I just ignore comments like that, but sometimes I get so angry, I tell them to shut up, and then I mutter something much worse to myself. "

—JOSH, 16

" Jessica and I were never great friends, but we used to hang out together sometimes. Last year we went to a music night at school together with another one of her friends. At first the three of us were fine together, but by the end of the evening, Jessica and her other friend had ditched me without even saying good-bye. I continued to call Jessica, but usually she wouldn't even bother returning the calls. The only time she would call me would be when she'd need something. Then she'd be all nice and sweet, saying something like, 'Do you want to come over to my house tomorrow? Oh, by the way, do you have the bio assignment?' **"**

—KIM, 16

DR. CHERYL DELLASEGA'S ADVICE ON BULLYING

Threats, shoves, freeze-outs, backstabbing, gossip, chatroom slams—so middle school, so young, but even in high school, some of this trickles on, sometimes poisoning friendships. Here's what Dr. Cheryl Dellasega has to say about bullying: "Some kids have learned early on that they can intimidate others with bullying behavior, and this gives them a false sense of power and control. They don't realize that fear is the basis of other kids' responses to them. Boys tend to be physical, usually out of anger and rarely within their circle of friends. They also tend to 'forgive and forget' (or at least forget) more readily than girls. Girls find it entertaining to start a 'drama' where one girl is targeted for exclusion and gossip by others. These kinds of behaviors often arise out of boredom, unfortunately. Sometimes people simply don't realize how they are interacting with their peers. They are truly shocked when the hurtful impact of their words is pointed out to them."

What can you do if a bully targets you? The answer depends, in part, on whether the bullying has been physical or emotional. If you are afraid the bully will hurt you or someone else, yell out something to get someone's attention, and get away—run if you have to. Getting badly injured really is worse than being temporarily embarrassed. Then make sure you report the incident to a school guidance counselor or a parent. If you've been bullied by someone, chances are the bully has done the same thing to others. High school students have stopped going to school because they've been afraid to run into a bully who has made them into victims.

If the bullying is more psychological than physical, here are some suggestions:

> Keep in mind that the bully is in the wrong, not you. Whatever the bully has said, try not to let it feel personal—it's not about you.
> Try to stay calm, or at least act as if you are. Bullies love to create distress in their victims. Take control of the situation by not appearing to be upset.
> Talk to the bully, if you can. Many kids would never be able to do this, but if you're one who can, go for it.
> Ask your friends to support you. Talking about your situation may allow you to come up with your own solutions.
> Ask family members, your guidance counselor, a coach, or a teacher for advice. Everyone has experienced bullying—find out what worked for them.
> Practice at home or with friends how you will act and what you will say the next time you meet up with your bully. The more prepared you are, the better the outcome.
> Act with confidence. Bullies are more likely to pick on kids who appear to be vulnerable in some way. So rehearse your best posture and a loud, clear voice.

What if your friend is the one who's getting bullied? Being a bystander and doing nothing might make you feel like a bully, too.

Instead, help your friend recognize that the bully is the one with the problem and that you're there to listen. Agree that the bully is a jerk—your friend needs to hear you say that. If your friend wants advice, offer it, and if she or he wants you to confront the tormenter and you're ready, willing, and able, go for it.

If you have a sneaking suspicion that you might be guilty of bullying behavior, you need to figure out why you are acting in a way that hurts others. Think about what's going on in your head and in your life that's causing you to act that way. Research on teens who bully shows that as high school progresses, their popularity drops. No one wants to hang around with bullies. So if you are bullying to try to keep your place at the head of the popularity line, think again: your technique will backfire, and you'll eventually be pushed way to the back of the line if your behavior doesn't change.

Wrap It Up: Scoring at Friendship

Okay, do you think you have this friendship thing in hand? Know where you are going? Able to fix a broken friendship, move away from one that's over, and step into one that's new? Try this quiz, and get your friendship score.

1. **You are swamped—math test tomorrow. Your fault—you left it to the last minute. Your friend calls crying and begs you to come over and help her deal with her latest (and not the last for sure) breakup with Mr. Wonderful. You:**
   a. Run right over. What's a D in math compared with your friend's pain?
   b. Tell your friend you're busy, you've heard it all before—time to just get over the relationship.
   c. Listen sympathetically for a half hour and make a plan to hear the rest after you have taken your math test tomorrow.

2. **You hear from a mutual friend that your best friend has been talking about you–and not very nicely. Some of your darkest secrets are now out there. You didn't see this coming. You:**
   a. Share a whole list of things your friend had told you in strict confidence.
   b. Tell your parents you feel really sick and stay home from school because you feel so devastated.
   c. Call your friend, tell what you heard, and ask what's up.

3. **You have a new love interest. You know you are boring your friend to tears because you just go on and on, but you can't help yourself. You:**
   a. Think, "Who cares?" You would do the same for your friend.
   b. Plan to do something together that has nothing to do with love.
   c. Stop seeing your friend so you can concentrate all your energy on your new love.

4. **You are really worried about your friend lately. There are lots of little things–looking really messy, no interest in doing anything, late for school, sleeping all weekend. Your radar is working overtime. You:**
   a. Talk to an adult immediately and get some advice and help for your friend.
   b. Leave your friend alone. Everyone goes through tough times.
   c. Talk about your friend's problems with your other friends.

5. **Your friend's team is headed to the state championships. Lots of extra practice time eats into your friendship time. You:**
   a. Feel really jealous inside but don't say anything.
   b. Find your own stuff to do. By the time the state championships are over, you'll be ancient history.

c. Understand that this is big stuff for your friend. Be there to share in the excitement and be supportive. Hey, if they win, you'll get to go to a cool party, and if they lose, your friend will need a sympathetic shoulder.

SCORING:
1. C is the best answer. You are making the time your friend needs while keeping what you need—study time—in first place.
2. C is the best answer. You should always give your friend a chance to explain: either to 'fess up, and then you two can decide what to do next, or to deny the gossip, and then you can decide the truth.
3. B is the best answer. A true friendship often lasts a lot longer than love, and anyway, there is always room for both in your life.
4. A is the best answer. Actually, you have no choice. Those warning signs can mean your friend is in deep trouble and needs more help than you can give.
5. C is the best answer. Friends share good times and bad, and they understand when life gets busy and crazy.

How'd you do? Bat a thousand? Then look forward to keeping some of your friends forever and making new ones wherever you go. But if your friendship score shows that some extra coaching is in order, recognize that not everyone is a natural. Practicing your skills is worth it—nothing can take the place of a few deep, true friendships.

Heart Smart

> " When my boyfriend and I broke up, at
> first I was fine. Like I cried, but I knew it
> was definitely for the best. But then I
> found out two weeks later from two of my
> friends that he had cheated on me, and I
> was so disgusted and angry. I, like,
> went into a state of hating guys almost,
> and it was just bad. "
>
> —BRIANNA, 17

Dating 101

If you're going with or seeing someone, that relationship could be anything from very casual to way serious. While formal dating—you know the old movie-and-dinner routine—still happens in some places, often the norm is group dating or hooking up at parties. For many kids, hooking up with or getting with someone doesn't necessarily even depend on having a relationship. "Hooking up" is defined differently by different people, so it could be anything from kissing to oral sex. Sometimes hooking up leads to a relationship, but not usually. Many kids view hooking up as behavior with no strings attached—no expectations, no commitment. The problem? Often one person is secretly hoping that hooking up will lead to something more, while the other involved individual just sees the chance to have fun.

> " Basically, no one in my high school dates. They either go out with one person or casually hook up once with whoever is available. "
>
> —MOLLY, 17

> " I don't want to hang around with people who say they're in a committed relationship and then hook up with someone else. That's just disrespectful and mean. "
>
> —MICHIKO, 16

> " I've been going with the same girl for about three years. My parents like her a lot. She has become part of my family and is treated like she is. "
>
> —MIKE, 17

WHAT'S THE ATTRACTION?

High school kids do get involved in real relationships where there is some kind of commitment, even if it's going to be a very temporary one. How important is physical attraction in a relationship?

" Physical attraction isn't everything in a relationship, but it definitely plays a role. Anyone who says physical attraction isn't important is lying. "

—JOSH, 16

" I think it's relatively important that the person I am going out with be physically attractive. Although she doesn't have to be even close to beautiful, I want the girl to take care of herself physically. "

—JUAN, 17

" I haven't really looked at anyone recently, because I've been with my girlfriend for three years. "

—MIKE, 17

" Physical appearance has never been important to me. I definitely need to date someone who is decent-looking in my opinion, but personality compensates for looks and is far more important than any physical quality. There were plenty of extremely attractive guys I would never date simply because I didn't like their personality. "

—CHELSEA, 19

People who enter into relationships where it's all about appearance quickly learn that there has to be more or the feeling will die. What do most of your friends look for in relationships aside from looks? Lots of things. Here's what some teenagers said:

> You shouldn't go out with someone just because you're bored or because you can get something from that person.

—SUSAN, 15

> It's important to enjoy being with the person you're going with. It shouldn't feel like a hassle.

—LASHAWN, 16

> The most important characteristic I look for in someone I'm going out with is that we have lots of attributes and interests in common. If we can't have a conversation, it would be very awkward. And much as I hate to admit it, that my friends approve of this person is really important.

—ANDREW, 17

> He has to be someone I can have an intelligent conversation with one moment and then talk about stupid stuff the next. And he needs to be funny. Good looks wouldn't hurt either.

—RACHEL, 17

In high school, I always liked the type of guys who were more clean-cut and respectable. I liked guys who did well in school and were involved in different activities. They also had to respect girls. **”**

—MEGHAN, 19

IF YOU DON'T HAVE A BOYFRIEND OR GIRLFRIEND

If your friends are seeing someone, many of them take the commitment seriously. And most enter into those relationships because they really care about the other person. If you've never been in a romantic relationship, don't worry. There's no set timetable for when you have to start going out. Some people start dating in middle school, others not until college.

“ I don't feel the particular need to have a girlfriend, because at this time in my life, I think it would create more stress than anything beneficial that would come from it. I'm a pretty shy person, so it is difficult for me to approach a girl in that way. **”**

—JEFF, 17

“ I'm waiting to have a boyfriend until I finish school, because they can be distracting, and school is more important. **”**

—HARPINDER, 16

** "** I'd like a boyfriend. I don't have one, because
I would need to be friends with him first,
and the guys I'm friends with I don't want
to date. **"**

—LAUREN, 17

If you're not dating yet but you'd like to, find ways to let the person know you're interested. While it might be very romantic to imagine that the person you have your eye on will magically find his or her way to you, that's more likely to happen in movies than in real life. How do you show people you are attracted to them? Here are a few techniques:

➤ When you're walking in the hall, look that person in the eye. It's natural to want to avert your gaze, so fight that instinct.

➤ Think about how you might look to other people. Your grandmother was probably right about this one: you never know who you're going to bump into. Wearing a stained shirt when you run out to the store makes it a sure bet that you'll meet the person you have a crush on. Don't overdo this attractiveness business; looking like you're going to the Academy Awards every day is just weird, not a signal that you want to meet someone.

➤ Find a way to sit near your crush in the cafeteria or some other public place, and then work up your courage to make a comment, nothing monumental—anything about homework, a teacher, even the weather will do.

➤ Make sure your positive attitude about life shows. Research indicates that people are attracted to those who seem like they're having a good time.

➤ Take a chance. Maybe the person you like already likes you or will like you when he or she gets to know you or finds out how you feel. Do something to get that person's attention. You might have to go a little outside your comfort zone to get things started, but if you don't and that person is shy, it's a guarantee that nothing will happen.

If in-person meeting is too scary, start a conversation through IMs. The advantages? The other person can't see you blushing, and you can delete part of a message and start over if you've begun to write something really off-the-wall.

WHAT ABOUT LOVE?

You may or may not call what you're experiencing in a relationship love. That word is usually reserved for a very special connection. Many high school students are reluctant to get involved in a committed, exclusive romantic relationship because they already have a complicated life—schoolwork, part-time jobs, sports teams, friendships, and chores. Many wonder how they can give a relationship the time it needs to flourish when they can't even get through all the homework they have.

While some high school romances turn into long-term relationships, even marriage, the likelihood of that happening is low. But that doesn't mean those relationships aren't important. Having a boyfriend or girlfriend can be fun and can give you practice in the give-and-take of relationships.

If someone is saying "I love you" because that person wants you to do something you don't want to do, run the other way. It's true that some people say "I love you" because at a certain point in a relationship it's expected or because one of them wants something from the other—possibly sex, but it could be commitment or a date to the prom.

How do you know when you're in love?

> Love is a feeling in which you can't wait to see this person every day, and the two of you have a great communication bond.
>
> —ANDREW, 17

" One factor in love is feeling that you'd do anything to make the other person happy, but not to the point at which you'd sacrifice yourself totally for the other person. If another person allows you to do that, then that person is not in love with you. "

—SHENIQUA, 16

" Being in love means that you can't live without the other person, and you love being with them and have feelings that are so strong that you can't put them into words. "

—WENDY, 19

" When two people are in love, they have a mutual respect for each other in the sense that they can accept the good and the bad, and still want to be with that person despite their faults. "

—LI-MING, 19

" When you're in love, you can be yourself around that person, feel comfortable and happy with who you are around them. They make you a better person or bring out the best in you. And you can never get enough of them. "

—KARYN, 18

INTERNET DATING

No doubt, you've heard the Internet horror stories, like the one about the teenage girl who thought she was getting together with a guy her age but ended up meeting up with a dangerous pedophile. But you've probably also heard about people who've met each other through online dating sites and gotten married. The bottom line is this: you really have no idea who you're talking to when you're on the Internet. The person you've had those great conversations with could be the greatest person alive or a scary psychopath.

Staying Safe Online

> Don't give out personal information, like what school you go to, your last name, or your address.
> Never let anyone use your screen name or password.
> Remember that someone you considered a stranger when you first met online is still a stranger, even if you've had lots of conversations over a period of a couple of months.
> Don't agree to meet someone you just know from online communication unless a parent or other adult is with you and you're going to be in a public place.

> It's too risky to go out with someone you meet online. The guy who says he's 17 could be 50.

—DANIELLE, 16

> I wouldn't date someone I met in a public chatroom. I like to see the person and know what they are like before dating them. Online, you never actually know what the person is like, and they could be acting completely different from who they really are.

—JASON, 19

I don't think I would ever go out with someone I met online. It's sketchy. I feel like if you can't meet anyone in person, then something must be wrong with you.

—JHUMPA, 19

Liking Your Friend's Date

It happens all the time. Your friend is going with someone you're attracted to. Maybe you were even interested before your friend was. Most teens agree that while your friend and this person are dating, she or he is off-limits to you. No matter how drawn you are to your friend's date, getting involved doesn't make sense—it's the perfect way to destroy a friendship.

But there are some scenarios that are a bit more complicated. Figuring out what to do is worthy of an SAT essay. Here are a few situations for you to think about and discuss with your friends. Better to know their views now than when you've already ventured into territory that should have remained out of bounds.

1. Your best friend and her boyfriend of ten months broke up a few weeks ago. The end of the romance was by mutual agreement, and they've remained friends. Now you're interested in starting something up. Should you?
2. You found out from a reliable source that the girl your friend has been dating for about a year has hooked up with other guys at parties over the last couple of months. Your friend is not someone you're very close to, and you've always been interested in this girl. You see her at a party when your friend is not around. Do you make a move?
3. Your friend's boyfriend broke her heart when he ditched her suddenly. Now he's starting to flirt with you. You're attracted to him, but you didn't like the way he ended the relationship with your friend. What action do you take?

There are lots of other possible situations you might find yourself in. Here's some advice from other people who have been there and done that:

> " Once a person is your friend, you shouldn't go out with her boyfriend. I wouldn't do it, because it would bother my friend, and then it's not worth it. "

—DANIELLE, 16

> " You don't want to put yourself into competition with your friend for a girl. But if they break up, you wait a while and talk to your friend to find out if it's okay for you to go out with her. If it is, I'd say, go for it. "

—VIRKRANT, 16

> " If I were interested in my friend's ex-boyfriend, I'd stay away for a little while after the relationship ended. I wouldn't even flirt. But once both parties involved have gotten over the relationship, you can try to get some kind of thing going. But be sure to check with your friend first, particularly if the breakup was a bad one. "

—LIZ, 16

" I've been attracted to my friends' girlfriends before. In my high school, most of the relationships only lasted for a couple of months. So if I liked someone, it didn't take too long for them to become single. I wouldn't go out with them if my friend has something against her— like she ruined him somehow. But most of the time, we dated within our circle of friends, and it wasn't uncomfortable dating someone that my friend already had. "

—JASON, 19

" I was attracted to my friend's boyfriend when I was in seventh grade. To this day, she hates me for stealing him. "

—KENDRA, 19

The Prom

In 2005, high school girls spent an average of about $380 on their prom, according to one survey, with boys spending about $450. That's a lot of money for one night. For girls, the greatest amount goes toward a dress, while tickets, food, and transportation typically eat up two-thirds of the boy's budget. While many seniors look forward to their prom all year, many don't go at all. Across the country, kids said a date was not necessary for the prom, with many attending with their closest friends. For safety reasons, many schools have curtailed prom activities, including prohibiting students from taking limos. Parents may like the prom even more than their kids do— it's a great photo op. For many, the buildup is more fun than the actual prom.

" I had realistic expectations for the prom. I knew it wasn't going to be a fairy tale, and I didn't stress out about anything, even when I was running late. I went with a group of friends and just had fun. "

—KENDRA, 19

" My high school prom was not fun. It wasn't like in the movies. It was just a regular dance. Also, the DJ never showed up, so we listened to CDs the whole dance. "

—JASON, 19

" My prom was pretty lame. I was really good friends with my date, and I had fun with my friends and getting dressed up. But when I left the prom, I realized it wasn't the greatest thing— it just wasn't that fun in general. "

—MEGHAN, 19

Sex Matters

Sex is a hot topic—for you, your friends, and your parents. Between your raging hormones and the extensive sexual imagery in movies, magazines, and songs and on television, you're probably reading, thinking, and talking about sex a lot. And the subject is much more complicated these days than when your parents were your age. You probably have lots of *what*, *when*, *who*, *where*, and *why* questions. Deciding whether to become sexually active, regardless of how you define that, is a big issue. And if you're already sexually active, that doesn't mean you no longer have to think about what to do in the future. Every time you're in a potential sexual situation, you have questions to ask yourself and decisions to make. For more advice on making big decisions, see pages 194–95 in Chapter 9.

WHAT AND WHEN

Statistics vary from study to study, but it's very clear that not everyone is doing it during the high school years. A 2005 report from NBC News and *People* magazine found that 13 percent of 13- to 16-year-olds say they've had sexual intercourse, while 12 percent say they've engaged in oral sex. Another study, a Gallup Youth Survey, found that a lower percentage of 13- to 17-year-old boys and girls had engaged in sexual intercourse in 2003 than in 1991.

Everyone differs on what "sex" is, with some including oral sex in their definition, and others not. More teens are engaging in oral sex because they think it's "safe" from STDs. But it's not! Here's what people said about this subject:

> I know two girls who had sex before their freshman year of high school because they thought that would make them cool. But that was actually so uncool.
>
> —LILY, 16

> Oral sex is not sex. It doesn't carry the same consequences. You can't get someone pregnant.
>
> —JAKE, 15

> **❝** Personally, I feel that high school students are too young to have sex, but if they're okay with it and safe, then I'm really indifferent. Before having sex, you have to think about using protection and being in a closed relationship. **❞**

—RUNEE, 19

> **❝** People should only have sex when they get married. **❞**

—CARLY, 16

> **❝** Not having sex until you're married is a noble goal, but for the most part, it's not realistic. **❞**

—GABRIELLE, 16

Ten Questions to Consider Before Deciding to Have Sex

1. Are you really sexually attracted to and in love with this person?
2. Are you prepared to deal with pregnancy or sexually transmitted infections (STIs), which might be the result of sex?
3. If you know that your parents think you're too young to have sex, can you deal with hiding your activity from them and their disapproval if they find out?
4. Are you making your decision in the heat of the moment, or is it something you've thought seriously about for a while?
5. Are you saying yes because you feel pressured to get it over with?

6. How well can you deal with a breakup once your relationship has become sexual?
7. How will you protect yourself from sexually transmitted infections?
8. Are you going against your own values and religious beliefs?
9. Are you thinking about sex because most of your friends are sexually active?
10. Are you thinking about saying yes because you're afraid the person you're seeing will leave you if you say no?

DEALING WITH CONSEQUENCES

While the teen birth rate has gradually declined in the United States since 1990, current statistics indicate that almost one million teens become pregnant every year. The National Center for Health Statistics estimates that 17 percent of current 15-year-old girls will give birth while they're still teens. Regardless of how people (males and females are both involved) deal with their pregnancy, that fact forever changes their lives. Research says teen girls who feel they have lots of life options ahead—in terms of education and careers—are less likely to get pregnant. And don't forget about the boy's role in this. Guys who recognize that "being a man" has nothing to do with getting a girl pregnant are less likely to be involved in sexual relationships that result in pregnancy.

" My cousin just turned 18, and he and his girlfriend who's 17 have a 6-month-old, and she just found out that she's pregnant again. She lives with her parents, who mainly take care of the baby. He gives them money for the baby and sees the baby a lot. He's not a stupid kid, but he dropped out of high school. It's such a waste. If he had waited, he could have been a great father. He's a father in the sense that he plays with his child, but he doesn't provide any sense of security or hope for the future. He says he's happy about having a child. He says he's a man. But his family is really disappointed in him. He clearly didn't learn a lesson from getting his girlfriend pregnant the first time, because then he turned around and did it again. **"**

—ELENA, 16

" I think high school kids should have sex only if protection is involved and they know each other really well. On the other hand, if they can wait, they should, because there are many serious consequences of sex. Just last year, I would see a new pregnant girl walking down the school hallways almost once a month. **"**

—BRIAN, 16

" Nothing makes me angrier than people being irresponsible when it comes to sex. If you're not willing to deal with the consequences, then you shouldn't have sex. **"**

—ALYSSA, 15

Expert Advice

Sheryl Scalzo is the assistant director of education and prevention at AIDS-Related Community Services, Hawthorne, New York. She has this to say about STIs.

You can't tell whether someone has an STI from just looking at them, or even looking at body parts. So if you're thinking about having a sexual relationship, consider that. In our education and prevention work, we stress building a good relationship and developing communication and negotiation skills through role-playing and discussion. While the only way to be absolutely sure you don't get an STI is through abstinence, it's important to talk and think about screening and prevention. At a routine visit to a gynecologist, you are not typically screened for the presence of STIs unless you specifically request it.

Sexually transmitted infections (STIs) can be an unwanted by-product of sex, particularly unplanned, unsafe sex. Today, STIs may be life-threatening and, at the very least, life-changing. If you're reading this book, you're smart enough to know that you can't tell whether someone has an STI by how they look. People who are infected might be great-looking or nerdy. They might be poor or rich. And they might be in the top or the bottom 1 percent of your high school class. According to the Centers for Disease Control and Prevention (CDC), about fifteen million Americans contract STIs each year, with nearly half being between the ages of 15 and 24, even though people this age constitute only one-quarter of the sexually active population. In 2000, fifteen thousand new cases of HIV infection and AIDS were identified in the 15–24 age range. It's something to think about, isn't it?

WHAT DO PARENTS THINK?

Do your parents know whether or not you're sexually active? Do they know what's happening at your high school? Many parents are very open about sexual matters and would be happy to discuss the subject with you. A recent study found that parents are the most popular source of sexual information. If you have parents who feel comfortable with this topic, ask them for information, and discuss your opinions with them. However, some parents are too embarrassed to have any discussion with the word *sex* in it, even with their mature teen kids. If that's the case in your family, think about another adult you'd feel comfortable talking to—maybe your doctor or a counselor. Nothing you say or ask about is going to shock them. And remember, they were once your age, too. The important thing is to get your questions answered and your concerns discussed.

" Parents subconsciously know, but they don't really want to know everything, particularly when it comes to sex. "

—JAKE, 15

" Parents know what's going on with us, because they were that age once. "

—GABRIELLE, 16

" Either parents know what their kids are doing and decide to ignore it, or they're oblivious to it altogether. Of course, there are exceptions. "

—MIGUEL, 17

SEXUAL ORIENTATION

The high school years are a time when you are figuring out who you are and where you fit in. Sexual orientation is a significant area of identity, but the relationship between orientation and behavior is not totally clear-cut. Because the adolescent years are a time of experimentation, you or your friends might engage in homosexual behavior and still consider yourselves to be heterosexual.

While people in your class may be generally pretty tolerant of those who are different, prejudice still exists around sexual orientation. Also, your family's cultural, religious, and ethnic background may have instilled very strong views on the acceptance of homosexuality. Where lack of acceptance by peers and family is extreme, gay and lesbian youth may find that their lives have become unbearable. The rates of suicide attempts and suicide among homosexual and bisexual young people are significantly higher than is the case for their heterosexual peers.

If you are gay, lesbian, or bisexual, recognize the toll intolerance may take on you. Seek out sources of emotional support at school or elsewhere. And if you're straight and have not been the most accepting individual, think about what your prejudice might be doing to one of your peers who just happens to have a different sexual orientation from you.

> My school generally has liberal attitudes toward homosexuality, and kids are relatively accepting. There is, however, an undertone of joking toward gay and lesbian students. But from what I can tell, they are comfortable being in this environment and do not feel threatened or maligned.
>
> —BRIAN, 17

> "I have a friend who I think is a lesbian. There are certain things that would bother me, like if she made a pass at me. It would be awkward."

—SARAH, 15

> "I don't usually have any clue as to who is or isn't gay or lesbian, and that's the way it should be. I had a friend a couple of years ago who was bisexual, and that was totally cool with me, but when she started hitting on me, I freaked out and kinda had to get away from her."

—YOLANDA, 17

> "I'm friends with people who are gay or lesbian. As individuals, they're generally not treated differently, but among males, there's a little bit of homophobia, which gets annoying, but it's contained. Maybe a guy will show an over-expression of masculinity."

—KEVIN, 16

> "I am bisexual. Some of my friends know, but most don't. I have a crush on one of my friends who might be bisexual, but I'm not sure. I don't want to approach her because I'm afraid that I might lose her friendship, and I don't ever want that to happen."

—NIKKI, 16

The Ugly Side

Love, romance, and excitement make up the pretty side of relationships. Harassment and violence are the ugly, often hidden aspects.
In the case of sexual harassment, you don't even have to be in a relationship to experience it.

SEXUAL HARASSMENT

An unwanted hand on your back as you walk upstairs from the
school cafeteria. An unwelcome comment about a private part of
your anatomy on the school bus. Sexual harassment is unwanted and
unwelcome sexual behavior, which may be physical or verbal. Girls
are the victims more often than boys, but boys, too, can be harassed.
And harassment can be from the same or opposite sex. Unfortunately,
studies indicate that 80 percent of high school students experience
sexual harassment in some form. Some report one occurrence, while
others say it happens almost every day. The fact is, sexual harassment
shouldn't happen at all—to you or to anyone else. Even one time is
once too often.

When kids experience sexual harassment in school, particularly
when it has a physical component, they may begin to dread going to
school, talk less often in class, or have trouble paying attention.

The numbers who engage in sexual harassment are surprisingly
high. A 2001 study of students in grades eight to eleven found that
a little more than half said they have sexually harassed someone at
some point in their school lives.

While sexual harassment wasn't taken very seriously years ago,
school officials and parents today are more likely to recognize and
understand that these behaviors should not be ignored. In the following examples, the behaviors are considered sexual harassment:

> ➤ Intentionally brushing up against you or touching you in a sexual
>   way
> ➤ Forcing you to kiss or do something else that is sexual
> ➤ Spreading sexual rumors about you
> ➤ Sending or giving you unwanted sexual pictures

> Unwanted pulling at or taking off your clothing
> Writing sexual messages about you on the Internet or on bathroom walls or lockers at school
> Spying on you in the locker room or bathroom at school

With the large number of students affected by sexual harassment, chances are that you or one of your close friends has been victimized. If it happens to you, what action should you take? Don't ignore it. Hoping that it won't happen again is wishful thinking. Even if you're not the target in the future, someone else is likely to be. Sexual harassers are not typically one-time opportunists. Since those who harass typically don't expect active resistance, surprise them by saying something like, "Don't ever touch me that way again," or, "I know that you wrote those comments about me in your blog, and I want them to stop right now." If the behavior continues, contact a school administrator, and indicate that you expect your report to be investigated.

Sometimes just naming an unwanted behavior is enough to stop it. The phrase *sexual harassment* carries considerable weight with school officials. Fortunately, many schools today have an anti-sexual-harassment policy. But if yours doesn't, gather a group of interested students to work with teachers and administrators to implement a policy of this type and make sure it gets enforced.

DATING VIOLENCE

The last thing you might expect when you're involved in a romantic relationship is violence. Unfortunately, it happens, and too often. Sometimes, the jealousy in a relationship is flattering—"Wow, he must really love me if he wants to spend every minute with me." But a little normal jealousy has crossed the line when you not only no longer spend time with anyone else, but also are afraid to. Many people in this situation are embarrassed, or they blame themselves—"If I hadn't pushed him into going with me to the movies, he wouldn't have shoved me." And boys (who can be victims, too) are more often even more embarrassed, since admitting they are in a relationship where they are getting physically hurt is so against the media image of the "strong, tough male."

It's hard not to believe the boyfriend or girlfriend who says, "It'll never happen again—I just wasn't myself" (or "I was drunk" or "I was so stressed" or "My parents have been pushing me too hard, and I just exploded"). A date who is violent is almost always sorry and promises to never be violent again. But, chances are, he or she will. If you've ever been violent, get help before you lose control again. Your anger and jealousy are not signs of a deep love, but of deep trouble. And if you're a victim, remember that you're not to blame. Get away. Talk to your parents, good friends, a school counselor, or an adult you trust, and let them get the help you need to end a relationship that will never get better, only worse.

> " Most people don't talk about dating violence. And when you hear about it, it's hard to know what to do, since you're just in high school. "
>
> —GREG, 16

> " Guys beating girls they're dating is more common than people think. People don't want to talk about it, but it's definitely happening. People are stuck in situations, and sometimes the victims feel responsible for what has happened. "
>
> —DAVITA, 16

BREAKING UP AND MOVING ON

Breaking up is never easy. It doesn't matter whether you're the one who wanted it to end or the breakup was someone else's idea entirely. Some relationships drift slowly downward before completely dying out, while others take a sudden plunge. It's always hard to get through it, particularly if you've been seeing this person for a long time, like six months, and you've gotten into a routine of spending time together and talking to each other about every big and little thing that happens.

> " Even though she wasn't the love of my life, or at least I hope she wasn't, it was still hard when she broke up with me. I liked going to parties with her, and I always had someone to hang out with. It was nice being part of a couple. "
>
> —RICH, 17

> " After my boyfriend and I broke up, it kinda put me in a mind-set that I couldn't really trust any guys and felt like all guys were the same and pretty much scum. "
>
> —EMIKO, 19

> " When my girlfriend broke up with me, I was a little upset at first but eventually got over it. Our relationship went back to the way it was before, because we were all in the same group, and we were forced together, and that made things un-awkward. "
>
> —JASON, 19

After a breakup, it's a good idea to give yourself some breathing time before jumping into a new relationship. It's okay to go solo for a while. Do things that you didn't have time for when you were so wrapped up in love. Rely on your friends and family to support you. And when you're ready, open yourself to a new beginning with a new person. While you might be tempted to compare this new person with your ex, try to move on with a clean slate.

6

Teachers, Tests, and To-Do Lists

> Last year, two of my friends tied my shoes to my desk while I was sitting in class. I didn't notice what was going on, but at the end of class, I tried to get up and fell on the floor. My friends just walked out, leaving me like that. My teacher was staring at me, wondering what was going on. 'Why are you guys still here?' he asked. I couldn't reach the laces, so another girl in class had to untie my shoes. Then I needed a late pass to my next class. I never wore shoes with laces to school after that.

—REBECCA, 16

Making the Transition to High School

For some, the transition to high school is a breeze; for others, it's slow torture. If you had a tough time in middle school or junior high, you have a brand-new opportunity to make friends, get organized, and set a schedule for studying. But you also have to become familiar with a new building, your assignments are more complicated, and you have new teachers to figure out and lots of new kids to meet. If possible, walk through the school ahead of your first day, particularly if your school is large or the layout makes no sense, which is not uncommon in high school. How could you possibly know that Room 262 is across the hall from Room 219?

> My older brother took me around before school started to show me where everything was, which helped somewhat. It would have been even worse, but I still got lost that first week of class. My art class was in a separate wing, and I just couldn't find it without the security guard's help again and again.

—KIMBERLY, 15

> Don't take classes with your older sibling's teachers, if you can help it. They will expect you to be exactly like him or her.

—BRAD, 17

> Don't overload yourself the first year. Gradually build up your tolerance for stress and hard work. If you freak out your first year, you'll find the rest of high school impossible.

—SHAHEEN, 16

Get involved in as many activities as possible—that's really how you meet people. Also, don't be afraid to hang out with people outside your junior high group. *Everyone* wants to make new friends, and making new friends is one of the most rewarding experiences in the world. Also, focus on academics, but not too much. High school, of course, is about academics, but it's also about finding out about your interests and having some fun along the way.

—ELIZABETH, 16

In ninth grade, students tend to become discouraged because the new workload is overwhelming and everything is intimidating. Many students don't realize how willing teachers are to provide individual help after or before school. Students should definitely take advantage of this.

—PHU, 17

Courses, Homework, Tests, and Projects

It's not just that there's more work in high school than in middle school, but the topics, complexity, and expectations are totally different. You have more complicated lab work in your science classes and lengthy term papers to write in history. You have to make decisions about the courses you'll take. Do you want to earn college credit while still in high school? That's possible with Advanced Placement

(AP) courses. Many colleges look favorably on students who take these challenging courses, but figure out what you can manage. Getting a poor grade in an AP course will not be as impressive as an outstanding grade in a regular class.

While you've taken standardized tests before, the SAT, ACT, and AP exams are on a different scale. Before you start to panic, remember that you're not going to be just thrown into these situations without any preparation. Your teachers, guidance counselor, parents, older siblings, upper-class students, special programs, and loads of books are resources you can and should count on for help.

HANDLING HOMEWORK

Everyone has an individual style for doing homework, with some more effective than others. By now you know what your homework style is. Do you keep your supplies and books together so you don't waste time looking for paper or your calculator? Do you wait until the last minute to get started on your assignments and then find that you're too tired to really pay attention? Do you recognize yourself in the following quotes?

" I procrastinate until the last possible minute, and when I finally get my work done at two in the morning, I promise myself I won't do it this way again, but I end up doing exactly the same thing the next time. "

—ERICA, 16

" I use an agenda book and write all of my assignments in it. I also use highlighters and neon-colored flash cards. For some reason, when the cards are neon-colored, I can focus and remember better. **"**

—ELANA, 16

Some students feel so pressured with everything they have to do that they're tempted to cheat on homework. Sometimes the elaborate schemes that students create take more time than just buckling down and doing the work.

" I'm in honors classes, and my friends and I have this arrangement worked out. I do American history homework, someone else does Spanish, and someone else does English, and then we trade. The greatest amount of cheating goes on in honors classes. We never cheat on tests, just on homework, 'cause there's so much of it. **"**

—JACK, 17

TAKING CLASS AND STANDARDIZED TESTS

By now, you've taken lots of tests—in-class exams as well as long, standardized tests. By the time you leave high school, you'll probably have ample experience with every kind of test, from essays to multiple-choice to open-book to oral exams. Each kind of test requires a different type of preparation. If you're going to have an oral language test, for example, make sure you spend some of your study time talking aloud. If your test will include an essay, be sure you know the material well enough to be able to answer the question with specific information. Unlike multiple-choice questions, essay tests won't have any clues to guide you. While many students cram the night before a big test, that's definitely not the best way to learn or remember material.

> " I make lots of careless errors on tests like the SAT, so I know to look over my test before handing it in when I have the time. "
>
> —LIZ, 16

> " I don't get anxious, because I know the stuff on tests and I study a lot. My aunt gives me little tests on each subject, and I know not to rush. Also, I pray, and that helps. "
>
> —JULIA, 17

> " When I feel somewhat anxious before a test, I usually take a break from studying to hang out with friends or play video games or do something else that's non-academic to relax. Sometimes, I'll also plan out my studying in as detailed a manner as possible, so that I feel like I can just follow my schedule and everything will work out. "
>
> —MARIA-ROSA, 16

> " For standardized tests, I had a couple of different tutors. I don't think they were helpful, because I always dreaded doing the assigned work and would barely do what they asked of me. But I did learn to read the questions first and then read the selection. This allowed me to know what to look for when I was reading. "
>
> —JASON, 19

Tips for Test-Taking

➤ For the SAT, ACT, and AP exams, take practice tests—lots of them. Bookstores, libraries, and guidance offices have copies of books with practice tests.

➤ Get your stuff ready the night before the test, so you're not scrambling in the morning trying to locate your scientific calculator, the right kind of batteries, and enough number 2 pencils.

➤ Make an outline for any essays you need to write.

➤ Take a quick break during a test if you're getting extremely anxious. Close your eyes, and take a few deep breaths.

➤ Spread out your studying, so you're not trying to do everything in one night. If you study in advance, you can ask your teacher for help with any concept you don't understand.

➤ Know how the test will be scored. You should know if you lose more credit for wrong answers than for leaving a question blank (that's true of the SAT Reasoning Test, for example).

➤ If you have time at the end of the test, check for careless errors. For example, make sure you didn't miss the words *not* or *except* in a question.

If you have a learning disability, be sure to find out what special testing conditions are available for you, such as extended time or oral tests or availability of computers. Figure out which strategies make the most sense for you.

> I was in middle school when my learning disability was first identified. Getting the diagnosis was a good thing because I now had an explanation for the problems I had been having in school since the third grade. Now I get double time on every test—not just the SAT, but even class quizzes. So many kids have a learning disability that it's no big deal. I know lots of smart kids, even students taking AP courses, who have a learning disability. I used to use my learning

issues as an excuse with my parents, but I don't do that any longer. I know that when I don't do well on a test or on my report card, it's probably because I didn't study enough. **"**

—JOSH, 16

PROJECTS AND PAPERS

The most important piece of advice about papers is to pick a topic that interests you (when you have a choice). If your teacher says that the whole class has to write about the causes of the War of 1812, well, that's it—that's your topic. But if you're given a list of fifty topics to choose from, pick the one that most intrigues you, not the one that's easiest to complete. When schoolwork is interesting, you're more motivated and bound to do a better job. Make sure you have access to enough material on your chosen topic. It would not be a good thing to find out two days before your paper is due that you just can't locate enough relevant information.

Create an outline of your paper before you start to write. Outlines are a great way to organize your thoughts and to make sure that everything that's relevant will be included in one place or another. It's much easier to modify the outline than to redo the paper once it's been completed.

Here are examples of projects and papers that some high school students found interesting:

" For my American history class, I picked the repeal of the Eighteenth Amendment, which was the end of Prohibition, as my topic, because it sounded like it would be interesting to write about. The Prohibition was a law that couldn't be enforced. And I wanted to find out why a law was passed in the first place that most people were going to break. Because the research was so interesting, writing wasn't nearly as painful as I thought it would be and I got a 96 on the paper. **"**

—CHENOA, 16

" In ninth grade, we had to write letters to put into a time capsule. When we're seniors, we're going to get our time capsules back, so we'll see what we were like at the beginning of high school. **"**

—ED, 16

" Our chemistry class was given a recipe for making chocolate chip cookies, all using chemical code. I learned something and had fun. And the cookies were delicious. **"**

—KIM, 15

" My most interesting class assignment was to create a product and produce a commercial in Spanish. It was great fun going to the in-school studio to film the commercial. And it was challenging, since it had to all be in Spanish. **"**

—ANDREW, 17

While lots of students start working on their papers just a day or two before they're due, starting earlier is much less stressful. Here's one high school junior's proven strategy for writing papers:

> " I try to start papers *before* the night before they're due and do a little bit at a time. I also try to finish early, so I can give it to my teacher to look over a few days before the paper is due. This is extremely effective and often helps me to get a better grade, because the teacher can point out what she is looking for if I haven't included something. "

—AMUN, 16

Teachers: The Best and the Worst

What makes a teacher memorable? Some do it by being a nightmare, making you count the seconds until you're out of their class. But others stay in your memory because they've changed your life for the better in an important way. If you're fortunate, you'll survive the bad ones without permanent scars and flourish with the great ones. It's also important to ask your brothers and sisters and friends which teachers they were impressed with. It might be possible to get into the classes that these people teach.

THE AWARD WINNERS

Great teachers are a gift. Usually, what you get from those special teachers is more than pieces of knowledge. They pass on life lessons in how to think and maybe even how to live. They help you get excited about learning, and every student wants to be in their classes. Let those extraordinary teachers know—in person or in a note—that they've made a difference in your life. Here's what some high school students had to say about their special teachers:

I learned an incredible amount from my art teacher, whom I've had for two years. When I compared my old sketchbooks and my current one, I realized what an unbelievable difference this teacher has made. This teacher is also very down-to-earth—we have real conversations with her, like about politics. And she gives us candy before vacations. 99

—LIZ, 16

66My global history teacher in tenth grade gave us interesting projects, like acting out trials. We read books that helped us understand different cultures. His class taught us not the facts, but more about how to think. 99

—WANGARI, 16

66My favorite high school teacher was my Spanish 4 teacher last year. She was a young, brand-new teacher who was incredibly nice and cared about her students. I loved the fact that she was not condescending and treated us and spoke to us like adults. She often asked for our input about class assignments. 99

—LIANG, 17

These Teachers Get a D-

High school students around the country had no trouble describing awful teachers. Sometimes it's an obvious lack of knowledge or a boring way of conveying information, but more of the time it was their poor attitude toward students that landed them in the nightmare category. These are the teachers who bully their students and abuse their power. If you are faced with someone like that at your school, talk to your guidance counselor or your principal. It's hard to learn when you're intimidated.

> My English teacher in tenth grade was probably not a bad teacher, but I always felt stupid in his class. He would call on me, and when I couldn't answer right away, he would announce to the rest of the class, 'Does anyone want to help Jake?' and that would make me so uncomfortable.

—JAKE, 15

> I really couldn't stand my calculus teacher, and she obviously felt the same way about me. One day, when I put my feet up on the desk next to mine, she asked me whether I was comfortable in that position. I knew she wanted me to remove my feet from the desk, but I decided to give her a hard time, just as she gave me every day. My answer was, 'I'm quite comfortable this way. But thanks for asking.' The class laughed, which made her furious.

—RICK, 18

My worst teacher is my chemistry teacher this year. He is absolutely the most boring man alive. His class is extremely easy and also extremely boring. He repeats everything about twenty times during lectures, and he is kind of oblivious to everything. He's just a really weird guy.

—SHOSHANA, 16

I love English, and I love books and discussing them. But the atmosphere was silent and awkward in this one class. The teacher would call on kids who didn't raise their hands. If you didn't give the exact right answer, he would embarrass you.

—CHARLOTTE, 16

I hated Mr. J. He's a stupid person. He tried to teach, but he just didn't know how. His examples made no sense, although maybe they did to him. No one actually understood what he was talking about. Then he would pick on me because he knew my name, but he wouldn't pick on the two girls who were actually doing something wrong.

—REBECCA, 16

My chemistry teacher assumed prematurely that everyone would be horrible. She would yell for no reason, even at me, and I got the highest grade in the class. She was just growly.

—ELLEN, 16

Stay After School—for Fun

Some high school students are involved in so many after-school activities, it's amazing that they have any time to do schoolwork or, for that matter, sleep. Others don't get involved in anything, until maybe the end of their junior year, when they realize that their lives on paper might not look great on a college application. While college admissions staff do care about those extracurricular activities, you're better off in the long run doing them because they're fun and interesting, not just because they'll enhance your college application. Here's what some high school students said about why they got involved in or dropped out of various activities.

I joined the theater group at school because I really like acting, but I dropped out because the people involved in it were mean. The teachers didn't try to get to know you unless you were one of the lead students. After three years, the faculty adviser still didn't know my name.

—ELANA, 16

" I've been in Girl Scouts since I was in kindergarten. It's fun and different from everything else I do. It has shaped me so much as a person. I've become more of a leader. "

—LIZ, 16

" I take a kickboxing class after school. It's fun, good exercise, and it's a good idea to have some idea how to defend yourself, particularly when you're like me—just five feet tall. "

—CHARLOTTE, 16

" I'm involved in my school newspaper, the school radio, the Young Democrats Club, tutoring, tennis, two diversity clubs, and a student ambassadors group. I am interested in journalism, which explains the paper; the radio was something my friends and I decided to try, and it ended up being very fun. I'm very interested in politics, so the Democratic club is an outlet for that. I love Spanish, so I tutor this one freshman in Spanish, and it seems to be helping him a lot. I play tennis during the fall, because it is the only sport that I really love and can actually play without looking crazy. The two diversity clubs are basically meant to help stop bullying and harassment and to promote tolerance. "

—PADMA, 16

> **"**I've been playing for my town's softball team for a couple of years. The team sucks, but last weekend, we won for the first time in two years. **"**

—CHANA, 17

> **"**I tutored at the public library and was on the varsity tennis team while I was in high school. I liked the tennis, but basically I did the tutoring because I knew I needed some community service to look good on my college applications. **"**

—JEFF, 19

Go to College or Put It Off?

One of the biggest decisions you'll face during high school is whether to go to college, and if so, which one and when. While some high school students elect to put off college for a year or so or not to go at all, many opt to continue their formal education right away without a break. Some who take a break do so for financial reasons, others because they barely passed their high school classes and can't imagine taking on a college-level program. Some students have opportunities to travel either with their families or as part of a teen program.

Research has found that while the overwhelming majority of high school students believe in the value of higher education, many don't pursue it because they think they can't afford it. If that describes you, you should know that most colleges will help you financially with loans, work-study programs, and outright scholarships based on need. If you really want to go to college, don't let finances stand in your way. Find a way to pursue your dream, instead of waiting for that dream to fall in your lap. The fact is that college graduates earn significantly more money in the long run than do high school graduates and have opportunities for jobs that are not open to those who haven't gone to college.

College Information Sources

➤ Parents, older siblings, and other relatives who've gone to college have their experience to share with you. Besides, they know your personality, interests, and grades.

➤ Teachers are generally willing to give advice, but you need to ask. You'll need teachers' letters of recommendation for many colleges, so asking for advice is one way for them to get to know you and your motivation better.

➤ The guidance office at your school and your guidance counselor have a ton of information available, and unlike what you can learn from your older relatives, their information is likely to be very current.

➤ College guidebooks are multiplying by the moment. Take a walk through a bookstore to see the many choices you have, search online for one of these books, or visit your school or local public library.

➤ Colleges will send you information about admissions requirements as well as material about the school itself. All have websites, and many have DVDs they're willing to send to potential students. If you can, visit colleges to get an up-front and personal view of college life, preferably while school is in session. Those visits help you refine your choices, both by eliminating some alternatives that are just not you and highlighting those that feel just right.

Expert Advice

Michael A. Tedesco is a guidance counselor at New Rochelle High School in New York. He offers this advice on choosing a college.

It's important to remember that there are many colleges that might be right for you, schools that offer a positive social life and a great education. Some students think that they must be worthless when they get rejected from their first-choice college, but that's just not true. Never apply because of the name or to compete with your friends—this just creates unnecessary stress.

> Not going to college has never been an option for me. I've known since I was five that I was going to college, basically even before I knew what college was. I knew that college was something you did to get a good job and be happy.

—BETH, 16

> My grades have been pretty bad all through high school. Since it's now the end of my junior year, it's really too late to turn things around. I'll probably end up at a community college and have to live at home. But if I do well there, I'll transfer to a school far away from home. That's really what I want to do.

—SUSAN, 17

> " When I began my college search, I did not want to deal with a hired college counselor. My parents, however, insisted that I see one throughout the college application process and basically forced me into his office. "
>
> —SETH, 17

> " The most important thing I did during my college search was to narrow down my choices, based on what I wanted, not on what everyone else said I should want. "
>
> —JAMAL, 18

> " College is about self-motivation and is a lot less structured than high school. College provides more spare time, so it's very easy to get carried away with socializing and extracurricular activities because you always think you have lots of time to study. "
>
> —KENDRA, 19

BAD GRADES, COLLEGE REJECTION LETTERS, AND OTHER AWFUL THINGS

No one can get through high school without a couple of big disappointments. While it's easy to forget some of your most successful experiences, you probably have a harder time letting go of the hurts.

Remember that even the best and the brightest have to deal with bad grades, rejections from their first-choice colleges, and not being picked for the school play.

> Last year, I worked really hard on my term paper in history, but I misunderstood what I was supposed to do and got a bad grade. So something that I expected to help my grade instead really hurt it.

—CARLY, 16

> When I wasn't picked to become a senior helper, I was pretty disappointed. That's a student who goes over to the freshman campus to help them get adjusted to high school. I remember feeling like, 'What's wrong with me that I didn't get it? Why did all of these other kids get it and not me?'

—ELIZABETH, 16

> At the end of the second marking period, my English teacher gave a test that covered material from the entire marking period. I really needed to raise my grade in the class and finish off strong so that colleges would see I was making a great effort. Following the test, I felt that I had done reasonably well. A few days later, however, when I was handed back the exam, I was horrified. I had gotten a 69. I basically gave up all hope of getting into a college I

really wanted to get into. It turns out that I had completely misread the test directions. I immediately felt extremely depressed and had never been so upset by a single grade. My teacher understood my mistake and fortunately was willing to curve my test grade. 99

—FAHIM, 17

66 Receiving my first rejection letter from a college was really upsetting and scary, especially since this was the school I really wanted to go to. Once I got the letter, I looked online and tried to find another school that was similar to this one. Now that I'm at this school, I love every minute of it, and my choice here was correct and exactly what I wanted. 99

—JASON, 19

Tips for Handling College Rejections

➤ Think about all the famous, successful people who were rejected from their first-choice college, and all the non-famous people you know (almost everyone) who received college rejection letters.

➤ Don't see the rejection as a personal rejection of you as a person. Many colleges are so competitive today that many admissions directors admit that as many as 80 percent of those who were rejected could have been successful at their school.

➤ Learn from the rejection. Perhaps the fit between you and the school you picked was not as good as you thought. The college admissions staff might have recognized from your application that you'd be better off somewhere else.

➤ Focus on the positive aspects of other schools you applied to. You should only apply to schools you really want to attend. Even your so-called "safety" school, the one you're sure to get into, should be one you view positively.

➤ If you are still passionate about getting into the college that rejected you, you might be able to transfer after your first year at another college. Keep that option in mind, although you probably won't have to use it, since you will most likely really like the college you end up going to and want to stay.

The academic skills and study habits you develop during high school can help you succeed in college and in your work life. Are you taking advantage of the opportunities that are available at your school?

Jobs, Internships, and Mentors

7

> " I volunteered at my town's summer camp. I liked being outside and around the kids. It feels good to be involved in my community. Little kids come up and give me a hug. And next year I was promised a paid job as a counselor. "
>
> MALCOLM, 17

In high school, everything costs more. Your school activities—sports, clubs, teams—have dues, equipment, costumes, and other expenses that selling candy bars and other fund-raisers don't cover. You have proms and class trips. Maybe getting a car is your big goal—and Mom and Dad aren't paying for it, or they'll get the car, but you need to cover insurance, repairs, and gas. You need clothes, not just for school, but also outfits for weekends, working out, going out. And you go out more—maybe on dates, maybe in groups—no matter, someone has to pay, and the kiss of death is to be labeled the moocher in the group. You'll find out soon enough that if you don't offer to pay when it's your turn, you'll be invited along less and less.

Maybe you're lucky and have such a generous allowance from your parents that it covers everything you need. Enjoy being in that group of less than 1 percent. Or maybe the stuff you do is really inexpensive, and you get by just fine. But most teens will find that when they hit high school, they need to start earning some cash.

Legally Employed

You probably know where you can and cannot work, but if you're not sure, the U.S. Department of Labor has a website called Youth Rules (youthrules.dol.gov). Here you'll find what jobs you can legally work and how many hours you can work at them per week. Here's a summary of the info from that site:

➤ Youth 18 years or older may perform any job, whether hazardous or not, for unlimited hours.
➤ Youth 16 or 17 years old may perform any non-hazardous job for unlimited hours.
➤ Youth 14 and 15 years old may work outside school hours in various non-manufacturing, non-mining, non-hazardous jobs. They may *not* work:
  • More than 3 hours a day on school days, including Fridays
  • More than 18 hours per week in school weeks
  • More than 8 hours a day on non-school days
  • More than 40 hours per week when school is not in session
➤ Also, 14- and 15-year-olds may not work before 7:00 A.M. or after 7:00 P.M., except from June 1 through Labor Day, when their permissible hours are extended to 9:00 P.M. Under a special provision, youth 14 and 15 years old who are enrolled in an approved Work Experience and Career Exploration Program may be employed for up to 23 hours during school weeks and 3 hours on school days (including during school hours).

States have different regulations from the federal government, as do jobs in agriculture. So check your state's department of labor website. Your local library or school library might have this information, too.

I work so I can buy things I like and not feel
guilty about spending my parents' money. I like
shopping and getting my nails done. It's good to
have my own money to do things with friends like
go to the movies and bowling.

—HEATHER, 18

JOBS YOU CAN DO

Under the federal government's age regulations, the jobs you can do
when you are 13 or younger are:

➤ Deliver newspapers
➤ Baby-sit
➤ Act or perform in motion pictures, television, theater, or radio
➤ Work in a business solely owned or operated by your parents
➤ Work on a farm owned or operated by your parents

When you turn 14, you can also work in a(n):

➤ Office
➤ Grocery store
➤ Retail store
➤ Restaurant
➤ Movie theater
➤ Baseball park
➤ Amusement park
➤ Gasoline service station

You generally may not work in:

➤ Communications or public utilities jobs
➤ Construction or repair jobs
➤ Jobs that require driving a motor vehicle or helping a driver

> Manufacturing and mining occupations
> Jobs involving power-driven machinery other than typical office machines
> Public messenger jobs
> Jobs in which you transport persons or property
> Workrooms where products are manufactured, mined, or processed
> Warehousing and storage jobs

When you turn 16, you can work in any job or occupation that has not been declared hazardous by the Secretary of Labor. Find a list of these on the Youth Rules website.

When you turn 18, you can work any job for any number of hours.

Is a Job Right for You?

If you want a job, talk to your parents or guardians. They may up your allowance if they realize you have a legitimate need for more money. If they can't, then know that studies show that kids who work long hours often get lower grades. So, you'll have to figure out how to manage your time—see pages 166–69—in order to maintain a good grade point average. You will also have less time for friends and for school activities. And after taxes are taken out, your part-time job paycheck will be less than you expect. So before you look, think very carefully about your reasons for getting a job and how important those reasons are. Make a list of pros and cons (see pages 172–73 for some decision-making help), and then show it to a friend, your parents, a teacher or guidance counselor, or other adult you trust. Also, talk to other kids who are working, and get their opinions. Instead of working during the school year, consider earning extra money during the summer and school breaks only.

> I was the dance and adventure assistant at a
> day camp last summer. Besides making money,
> it was something to do instead of just sitting
> around being bored all summer. I had a chance

Five Rotten Jobs

The National Consumers League published a list of the five worst jobs for teens. You may make money, but working in these jobs isn't worth the risks.

1. Driving and delivery, including operating or repairing motorized equipment
2. Working alone in a cash-based business or late at night
3. Cooking with exposure to hot oil and grease, hot water and steam, or hot cooking surfaces
4. Construction and work at heights
5. Traveling youth crews, such as selling items door-to-door

---

to meet new people, and I became better friends with people I already knew. The job taught me to be more responsible and to manage my time. I even managed to finish my summer school assignments without a problem. The job wasn't easy, because I was working with kids ages 3 to 7, but it was fun. And I'm looking forward to being a senior counselor at the same camp this summer. 99

—LIZ, 17

YOUR RÉSUMÉ: ALL ABOUT YOU

When you apply for a job, you will want to have a basic résumé. Even if all the jobs you apply for have applications, creating a résumé helps you keep your work and volunteer experience and other information straight. Plus, including a résumé with the application is impressive. Here are some tips for putting together a businesslike résumé:

> Even if you haven't worked, include your volunteer activities, unpaid jobs such as baby-sitting your little sister, and any special awards you may have won as a Boy Scout or Girl Scout or in school or sports.

> List your technical and computer skills. Include your grade average if it's high (at least a B+ or 85).

> Make sure your résumé fits on one page and is easy to read. Check it for spelling errors, and don't rely on spell-check to catch the mall. (Yes, it should read "them all"!)

> You can find many examples of résumés online or at your local or school library, or ask your guidance counselor. Look for a template specifically made for teen résumés.

AT THE INTERVIEW

Prepare some questions in advance of your interview, and practice answering them. Try to get some information about the place of business: talk to an employee, or look up the company online. Get some rest the night before. Make sure your outfit is washed and ready and fits well. Shine your shoes. Don't be late. Make sure your first questions aren't when you get paid, how much you get paid, and how many vacation days you get! Ask about the kind of work you would be doing and the skills the employer is looking for. Use your answers to demonstrate how your skills and experiences are a good match. Try to appear confident. Most people are very nervous in a job interview, but the successful job seeker is the one who shows it the least. The better prepared you are, the less nervous you will be.

Listen to what the interviewer is saying, and answer honestly and completely the questions you are asked. It is better to ask the interviewer to repeat a question (hey, interviewers understand that you are nervous) than to ramble on about something that was never asked.

Getting Your First Job

Kelly Whalen is the assistant director of recreation for the town of Washington, New York. She hires lots of teens for part-time and summer jobs. Here are her top five tips:

1. Come in and ask about the job yourself. Don't send your parents in to pick up the job application!
2. Make good eye contact. Look pleasant. Speak clearly—no mumbling and uh-huhs.
3. Dress neatly. Be clean. Look respectable. You don't have to wear a suit to apply for a summer recreation job, but you shouldn't wear short shorts or ripped jeans either.
4. Have checkable references—and none should be members of your family. I always check references, so don't think they won't be checked.
5. Remember that your grades and extracurricular activities are important.

Kelly also offers this advice: "If you don't get the job, ask if there is other work you can do. Can you volunteer? Can you do an internship? Sometimes teens quit or don't work out. I'll remember who was enthusiastic and sounded as if he or she really wanted the job, and I may be able to offer something after all."

Questions to Ask in an Interview

➤ What would a typical workday be like?
➤ What skills and abilities are needed in this job?
➤ How can a person do this job successfully?
➤ What are you looking for in a candidate? (Listen and then follow up with a statement that shows how your work experiences and abilities match what the employer is looking for.)

Kelly's Tips for Keeping Your Job

1. Always be at least ten minutes early.
2. Don't be the first one out the door.
3. Don't bring your personal life to the job. You may have been out until 2:00 A.M. the night before, but don't talk about it and don't let it show.
4. Be enthusiastic.
5. Do what you're supposed to do—and then do some more.

Before you leave, thank the interviewer for his or her time. A few days after your interview, send a follow-up note or e-mail, or call the person who interviewed you, and let him or her know you are still very interested in the position. Thank the interviewer again for the time and information you were given about the job. Mention a specific aspect of the job you found intriguing, or note a personal quality that makes you a great match for the job.

SOME PLACES TO LOOK FOR A JOB

No family business to turn to? Check the classified section of the local newspaper. Walk around town, the local mall, or nearby communities with plenty of shopping; lots of stores hire extra help during the holiday season. Start looking in March or even earlier for summer jobs. Check whether your community has a job registry for teens. Ask your school guidance counselor about job postings. Talk to friends, your parents' friends, teachers, adults at your house of worship, coaches, youth group counselors, neighbors—spread the news that you are job hunting. Internet sites list jobs. Look for ones that specialize in work for teens.

Or create your own job. You can start your own business. You may make more money baby-sitting, caring for pets, doing lawn work, fixing computer glitches, teaching piano, or creating birthday parties for kids than you make working at the mall jeans store. To start thinking of ideas, fill out the Business Idea Worksheet.

Business Idea Worksheet

List your skills and qualities and the needs in your community.

Skills I Have

Examples: Technological, technical, mechanical, artistic, musical, and so on.

_____

_____

_____

Qualities I Have

Examples: Good with people, good communicator, patient, children love me, strong, lots of stamina, and so on. (If you can't think of many, ask your parents or a friend for help.)

_____

_____

_____

Needs in My Community

Examples: Dogs need to be walked during the day while adults are at work; lots of younger kids need tutoring.

_____

_____

_____

After you've completed your lists, brainstorm some business possibilities that match your skills and qualities with the needs of your community. What kinds of businesses can you start?

Make a flyer and some business cards, and post them throughout your community. Get a parent's okay first, and check your town regulations about posting flyers. Only take on work you can handle. And make sure your prices are fair. Don't charge so much that no one hires you, but don't charge so little that you are practically working for free.

> " When I started a software business in high school, I had high hopes for it, but all I got was charity work from my parents and my friends' parents. My downfall was that I didn't know about advertising, so no one knew about my business. The experience wasn't a total loss. Although I didn't make much money, I learned how to get a post office box, register the business in my state, and start a website. "
>
> —ROB, 19

Tryouts: Getting an Internship

Sometimes the best work is unpaid. Internships allow you to try on a job or two. Fashion design may be your dream until you do an internship and realize that most graduates don't become world-famous designers but instead are anonymously designing ready-to-wear blouses by the dozen for a chain of stores. Or you have visions of your huge desk floating in the executive suite of a Wall Street investment bank—until you find out about the years of working hundred-hour weeks to get there. So internships can open your eyes, give you a dose of reality, and let you make a little splash without taking a dive into the pool.

Five Questions to Find an Internship Match

1. What are your best school subjects?
2. What hobbies do you have?
3. What causes are you passionate about?
4. What types of careers interest you?
5. What are your top skills: math genius? computer whiz? artistic talent? socially blessed? athletically inclined? organizationally gifted?

Internships look great on a résumé or college application, so if you can afford to work without pay, try one on. Start with your high school guidance counselor. Two books to look at are *Peterson's Internships* and *The Internship Bible*. Ask your local library for help, too.

Go to websites such as idealist.org (see pages 200–01), which lists internships in the not-for-profit world. The following sites also are helpful:

> ➤ internshipprograms.com
> ➤ internabroad.com

Your local paper, especially a weekly that has lower ad rates, may also list internships. Network: again, let the adults in your life know you would like to do an internship. If you know someone working in a field that interests you, you may even be able to structure your own internship—after all, you are working without pay. Are you savvy in Web design? Check out graphic design firms in your area. Interested in the environment? Speak with administrators at your local parks, nature centers, or botanical gardens.

To apply for an internship, do just as much preparation as for a paying job. See the tips on page 157. Prepare a résumé and a set of questions for the interview, and follow up with a phone call or thank-you letter or e-mail.

What You Can Learn from Working

When you land a job or internship, you may be lucky enough to discover the job you want to have forever, or—like most people—you may work at many jobs and cross them off your list of jobs to never do again. A survey conducted by the Harris Interactive Youth Query asked teens what were their top ten most prestigious occupations and professions. Can you list your top ten? See if they match the following answers:

1. Doctor
2. Member of Congress
3. Military officer
4. Firefighter
5. Scientist
6. Actor
7. Police officer
8. Athlete
9. Lawyer
10. Entertainer

Why do you think these professions made the top ten? Could it be more about money and being famous and less about doing what you love?

The list changed when the teens were asked which job they would most like to have. The top eight professions were:

1. Doctor
2. Teacher
3. Actor
4. Engineer
5. Entertainer
6. Athlete
7. President of the United States
8. Scientist

How many of those jobs do you think are realistic? How many actors do you think are able to make money through acting alone (and not also tending bar or waiting tables)? Not many. How many people become president of the United States? Hmm—one every four years is not that many, but you can use an interest or talent in the acting field or in politics in a variety of related professions. How to discover them? Look for a mentor.

Finding a Mentor

A Web-based resource for finding a mentor is a site called icouldbe.org, through which skilled professionals provide mentoring and career-planning tools to high school students. It was founded by Adam Aberman, a high school teacher who saw that kids tuned out when they didn't see the relevance of what they were learning to their lives and their futures. He thought if he could use technology to connect teens to mentors in a safe environment, teens could build on their own strengths, identify career paths, and get real-world advice and concrete tools along the way. E-mentors help people like you visualize where you want to be and then work backward through the steps you would need to take to get there.

Jobs, mentorships, and internships are all good things to add to your busy high school life. But where do you find the time with everything else you are doing? Keep reading. The next chapter offers you tips on how to fit it all in.

Benefits of Mentors

Adam Aberman, the executive director and founder of icouldbe.org, has this to say about finding and using a mentor.

Mentors can't make decisions for teens, but they can help teens learn more about themselves, sift through millions of plans and ideas, see how big the world is and all that they can do, build confidence, become a better writer and a clearer thinker, learn how to gather and get the info they need to succeed, and learn what they would really be doing in the job of their dreams. For example, they can answer, "How does a lawyer or a graphic designer spend her day?"

If your school doesn't offer e-mentoring through icouldbe.org, you can go to the National Mentoring Partnership website and try to find links near your community. Look at the people closest to you: Who do they admire? Who do they trust? Could one of those people be a mentor to you? You could plan a little script: think of how you could approach someone to help you out or get some advice with your career planning. Conversations with mentors can be formalized or very informal. You can meet regularly or just once or twice.

Finding a mentor isn't easy—there is no number you can call. But it's worth it. I have a success story I often share. A teen's parents were immigrants and knew little about the American educational system and could give no advice on college. She wanted new experiences, wanted to learn, and wanted to go to college. Through her mentor at icouldbe.org, she learned about the college her mentor had gone to, applied, and was accepted and was very successful.

The biggest success is when someone had a mentor and then turns around and becomes a mentor herself.

8

Manage Your Life

> " I'm a big list maker. I like to cross off what I've done. Then I can schedule something fun. "
>
> —JULIA, 17

Okay, friends, family, school, work . . . what about everything else? What about a car? What about free time? How do you fit in everything you need, want, have to do? How do you decide what you want—and how do you get there? This chapter will give you advice and tools to manage all parts of your life.

If Procrastination Were a School Subject, You'd Be Making As

11:00 P.M.—You've IMed all your friends. You've searched the Net, downloaded some music, eaten a late-night snack, and seen the parents to bed. But you're still only one page into your English paper—and most of that page is the title written in *really,*

really big letters. You know you need sleep (see page 3), but maybe you'll get an hour or two a night at the pace you are living. Which isn't good. Which makes getting your work done harder. Which makes doing well in your sport almost impossible. Which makes you grumpy, jumpy, irritable, and just no fun to be around.

Procrastination is a bad habit that's hard to break. Most everyone—except those super-organized gurus you see on TV (who most likely have personal assistants to keep them on track)—puts off stuff that isn't fun to do. It's so easy to sit at the computer to do your homework and be sidetracked into e-mailing your friends or downloading some music.

Time Control

You know you have twenty-four hours in your day. So what you need to figure out is how to use those twenty-four hours most effectively. You want to think of time in the same way you think about money. They are both resources that you spend to get what you want.

Where Does the Time Go? First, figure out how your time is spent during a normal school year week. For each activity, do the math:

Hours per Day × How Often Each Week = Weekly Total

➤ Classes at school
➤ Homework
➤ Sports
➤ After-school clubs
➤ Youth groups
➤ Job
➤ Hobbies: music, dance, etc.
➤ Sleep
➤ Time on computer or watching TV
➤ Time talking with and IMing friends
➤ Hanging out with friends
➤ Eating
➤ Time with family

What did you discover? Did your weekly activities take up more hours than the 168 hours that are in a week? If you have the power to stop time, you're okay. But, if you're the typical human teen, you need to figure out a way to manage your time.

> The first thing I do when I get up is think about all the things I have to do that day, so two seconds before my softball game after school, I'm not running around the house. I have trouble keeping my calendar up-to-date, and I wish I were better at it, because I think it would help keep me on track.

—JULIA, 14

TOP FIVE TIME MANAGEMENT TIPS

1. Make a To-Do List. Keeping an up-to-date to-do list makes sure you don't forget important things and helps you prioritize your tasks.

To-Do Lists That Work

➤ A good to-do list is like an outline for a school paper. Bigger tasks are broken into smaller parts. Do that until you have a true list of all the things you need to do.

➤ Put the tasks in the order they need to be done. What has to be done before another task? What are your closest deadlines? What tasks have the biggest or worst consequences if they aren't done on time?

➤ Look at your list. Are there any tasks you can cross off right away? Decide if you need to do everything on your list.

➤ Look at what's left, and give each task a realistic end date.

➤ Cross off each task when it's done. Rewrite your list—daily, weekly, whatever works best—putting new tasks in the right order and giving them the right priority.

2. Multitask. Use time when you are waiting around—for a bus, the dentist, the start of classes, your chronically late friend—to read, reorganize your to-do list, study, make your essential phone calls. Carry a schoolbook, planner, and phone with you to take advantage of those extra minutes. Plan ahead—how can you accomplish more in less time? If you have two reports due, can you pick topics that would allow you to research both simultaneously? (For example, a report on Elizabethan England for your history class would overlap a report on Shakespeare for English.) If you need to go to the library, what else can you accomplish while you are there?

3. Put Yourself on a Strict Time Budget. You have set your priorities. You know how you want to spend your free time. Stay within your time budget; don't let your mind wander or get distracted so that tasks take longer than they should. If you're online to collect information for a science report, don't decide to download some music.

4. Say No. Saying no to friends, family, your boss, or coach is hard—and sometimes you can't say no, and you'll need to adjust your schedule for the unexpected things that crop up each day. But when you can say no—especially if you are someone who always says yes and everyone comes to you for favors and help because you always *do* say yes—hey, it's time to stop saying yes all the time. Practice saying no in front of a mirror. Know that your friends will still be your friends if you say no to them some of the time.

Your family will understand if you have a good reason to bow out of an activity or task—just give them some notice. "Mom, could I not go to Grandma's on Sunday? I have to work on Saturday, and I have a test on Monday that I need to study for on Sunday." Of course, if you blow off your studying and shoot to the mall with your buds, expect your family to be really unhappy and not trust you the next time around. But if they know you are using your time responsibly, they'll respect how you have planned to use your time.

5. Stop Worrying. Getting upset, fretting over what you have to do, and feeling overwhelmed are monumentally unhelpful. If you feel as if you are staring up a mountain of stuff to do, figure out one small step from your to-do list, and just get it done. You will definitely feel better.

My Life Is in Such a Rut That I Can't See over the Walls

Sometimes you procrastinate because you are just plain old bored. You and your friends do the same thing, talk about the same people, watch the same shows again and again and again z-z-z-z-z . . . oh, excuse me, I must have nodded off. Only you can climb out of the deep rut you have made.

STEP 1: DO SOMETHING DIFFERENT

Thinking of something different to do isn't hard, is it? But actually doing something different—that's much harder. Ruts are really comfortable, and human beings like to stay within their comfort zones. So maybe do something a little bit different. Don't exercise? Start walking for fifteen minutes a day. Never kept a journal? Try keeping a blog or writing in a journal a few minutes a day. You and your friends listen to the same music? Download a new style of music into your iPod. Need some help figuring out what to do next? Find a mentor (see pages 163–64).

STEP 2: FIND YOUR MOTIVATION

Look at your to-do list. What could you accomplish that would make you the happiest? How can you arrange your schedule to get that done first?

STEP 3: MAKE A DREAM TO-DO LIST

What would be your dream to-do list, a dream week of tasks? Write down this imaginary to-do list, and then set some SMART goals to make some of those dreams come true.

SMART Goals

➤ **Specific.** Break your goal into small steps, not huge wish lists. Define what you are going to do and how you will get there. "I want to _____. To get there, I need to do 1. _____, 2. _____, 3. _____, etc."

➤ **Measurable.** "I will be really good in sports" is not measurable. "I will improve my pitching by practicing four hours a week for four weeks" is. Make each of your steps to reach your goal measurable.

➤ **Achievable.** Your goal should be realistic and doable. You shouldn't set a goal to be the winner of "American Idol" if you croak instead of sing. Your goal shouldn't cost so much money or so much time that it can't be done, and it shouldn't require resources that you don't have or can't get. Use some realism when deciding what to do; don't expect your goals to be like the candles on a birthday cake. Goals need effort, not wishes.

➤ **Rewarding.** Your goals should be in line with your values and should benefit you and/or others. If academic achievement is very important to you and your family, then a goal to improve your grades or work toward a scholarship fits. If you feel strongly about the environment, a goal to get an internship with an environmental action group also fits. Don't feel pressured to set goals that don't suit you. If you love acting and set a goal to try out for a community theater group, don't let friends—who may feel threatened by your dedication—deter you. On the other hand, sometimes friends and family can push you to think in new ways and set goals that are a bit outside your comfort zone. You may never have the nerve to try out for a school play, but if all your friends are willing to take that chance, they may encourage you to try out, too—and you may discover a new talent and a new passion.

> **Time-specific.** You should know when you have reached your goal. That means your goal is something that can be completed by a set date. "I will become more organized" is way too open-ended. "By the end of this month, I will have updated my planner and recorded all my deadlines and activities on my computer's calendar" has an ending date.

STEP 4: CELEBRATE

Make sure you celebrate your accomplishments—little ones like crossing off items on your to-do list and big ones like winning an award at school or reaching a major goal. Celebrations can keep you motivated by giving you something to look forward to. Celebrations can be small—getting a new book from the library and spending an hour reading it or taking a break and e-mailing a friend—or big. After a summer of walking four times a week, you might buy yourself some exercise equipment to use indoors in the winter months.

STEP 5: REACH HIGHER

Maybe you need to do more than just something different; maybe you need to push yourself to achieve greater things. A motivational quote reads, "Don't limit your challenges, challenge your limits." Think beyond what you usually do and what you feel you are capable of doing, and move forward.

Let the Force Be with You

Setting goals is mixed in with making decisions. Choosing a goal or picking a next step when you have many choices is hard. But, there are two tools used in the business world that can help you. You also are confronted with other types of decisions, such as feeling pressured by friends or the media to do things you may feel are wrong or you feel uncomfortable with. For more on that, see pages 184–89 in the next chapter.

BUSINESS TOOL #1: WEIGHING THE PROS AND CONS

The first is a tool that helps you uncover the pros and cons of a decision. It is especially helpful when you are thinking about making a big change. For example, you may have planned all along to go away to college and get a general business degree, but a summer job in the office of your local medical group has you intrigued by your local community college's two-year program in radiology.

Pros and Cons Chart

Change: Enroll in a two-year radiology program at the local college.

PROS	CONS
Lower expenses by living at home	Living at home—miss out on dorm life
In just two years, can get a job in field	Fewer career options—stuck in one program
Felt excited when working with radiology technician	Parents think I need four-year degree
Growing field—easy to get a job	Bachelor's degree is more prestigious
Not that interested in business classes	All my friends are going away
Won't have student loans to repay	

Next, assign a number to each—from 1 (the weakest) to 4 (the strongest). You might decide that your friends going away is a weak reason (a 1). Depending upon your financial circumstances, you might consider all the choices that save money to be the strongest (4s). Add the numbers in each column. If one column totals much higher, that column is pointing you in the direction to take.

Use the blank chart to analyze the pros and cons when you have to decide whether to do something big.

Pros and Cons Chart

Change: _____

PROS	NUMBER	CONS	NUMBER
_____	_____	_____	_____
_____	_____	_____	_____
_____	_____	_____	_____
_____	_____	_____	_____
_____	_____	_____	_____
_____	_____	_____	_____
_____	_____	_____	_____
_____	_____	_____	_____
_____	_____	_____	_____
TOTAL: _____		TOTAL: _____	

BUSINESS TOOL #2: ANALYZE YOUR OPTIONS

When you have to make a decision that has many good alternatives, this second business tool is better to use. For example, suppose you have saved enough money to buy a car and have narrowed it down to three choices. Creating a chart of your options can help you pick which of the three cars is best for you. First you list your options and your considerations in making a decision. In the sample option analysis chart, the options are listed down the left, and the considerations across the top. Then you decide the importance of each consideration. In the sample chart, "cost" is the most important consideration, so it gets a 4, while "fun to drive" is the least important, so it gets a 1.

Next, score each consideration on each option on a scale of 1 to 3, with 3 being the highest. In the sample, the best cost (lowest price) is for your uncle's sedan, so it scores 3. That car is the least fun to drive, so it scores just 1 in that category. After that, you multiply each score by its consideration rating. So, for example, your uncle's sedan scores $4 \times 3 = 12$ for cost, $2 \times 3 = 6$ for safety, and so on. Finally, for each option, add all these scores to get your total score for that option. For your uncle's sedan, $12 + 6 + 9 + 1$ gives you a total of 28. The highest-scoring option is your choice. And the winner is . . . the sedan this time. The five-year-old sedan scores the highest because it meets your considerations the best.

Sample Option Analysis Chart

THREE CAR OPTIONS	CONSIDERATIONS				
	COST (4)	SAFETY (2)	RELIABILITY(3)	FUN(1)	TOTAL
1. Uncle's five-year-old four-door sedan	3	3	3	1	28
2. A three-year-old compact car	2	2	2	2	20
3. A nine-year-old SUV	1	1	1	3	12

Use the blank option analysis chart whenever you have to make a tough choice from several options. If you have more than three options or four considerations, add more lines to the chart.

Option Analysis Chart

OPTIONS   CONSIDERATIONS

                   ___ (_)   ___ (_)   ___ (_)   ___ (_)   TOTAL

1. _____   ___   ___   ___   ___   ___

2. _____   ___   ___   ___   ___   ___

3. _____   ___   ___   ___   ___   ___

Need It, Want It, Gotta Have It

Decision-making tools can also help you manage your money. According to a study by Teenage Research Unlimited of Northbrook, Illinois, teens as a group spend over $155 billion a year, with average spending of close to $100 a week for each teen. But when the federal government surveyed teens on basic money management skills, half of them failed. So, before you spend your money on stuff that gets tossed or wind up in continuous debt to your parents, learn a few smart money skills.

When money comes in—be it from an allowance, a job, or some other source, save part of it for the big expenses. Keep it in a bank account, or have your parents save it for you. In 2005, about three-quarters of 13- to 18-year-olds had savings accounts, and about 16 percent had stocks, according to a survey by Junior Achievement and the Allstate Foundation. About 200,000 people like you across America have prepaid credit cards. With this kind of card, parents decide how much cash to put on the card, and each time you make a purchase, that amount is debited from the card. Because there's an itemized online account listing, you and your parents will both get to see how the money's being spent, which could be good—or not.

Navigate the Mall

Hitting the mall? We have mall crawling down to an art form, so read on. This advice comes from Kelly White, executive editor at GL.

GL's Ten Greatest Shopping Tips

1. Try before you buy. Sure, trying stuff on can be a pain—but dealing with returns is even worse. Running back to the store to stand in line at the customer service counter? Not fun. So hit that dressing room!

2. Bring a bud along. It always helps to have a second opinion right at your beck and call. Invite your most honest shopping pal—the one who isn't afraid to tell you, "Those pants make your butt look the size of Montana."

3. Hit up the clearance racks. When department stores are ready to bring out new merchandise, they'll sometimes practically give last season's merch away. Just be careful of sizing. Don't spring for those groovy pants in petites if there's a good chance you might shoot up five more inches before next winter.

4. Look for knockoffs. It's hard to afford designer duds on a shoe-string allowance. Flip through fashion magazines, taking partic-ular note of the trends you like, and go to discount stores for similarly styled items.

5. Splurge on basics. Saving money on fads that will likely go out of style in the blink of an eye is fine, but you should spend a little more to ensure lasting quality for classic items. Every girl should have a nice shirt, black pants, and a good pair of black flats. For guys, a good-quality button-down shirt, a pair of khakis, and a good pair of leather shoes work for many casual or dress-up occasions.

6. Find discount outlets. Search nearby shopping areas for boutiques that buy out the leftover stock from other stores. If you really do your detective work, you can score fine threads for a mere fraction of the original price.

7. Go thrifting. Don't shy away from thrift shops. Yes, most of the clothes have been worn by someone else, but you can get some real vintage gems at stores like Goodwill and Salvation Army for a steal. Just wash or dry-clean, and it can be as good as new (better even).

8. Don't lose that receipt. Even if you love an item and have no intention of returning it, you should hang on to your sales slip. What if the seam suddenly unravels? What if your best friend buys you the same exact shirt for your birthday? You could unexpectedly need to take it back, so keep that receipt for at least thirty days.

9. Accessorize. You can't live on clothes alone. Think earrings, belts, scarves, and . . . shoes, shoes, shoes! After you've picked out the outfit you're going to buy, think about how you're going to round it out.

10. Have fun! Hitting the racks shouldn't be stressful, so be sure you've discovered the joy of shopping. Remember that some days are better than others. If you're not having luck finding anything cute, chances are you'll spot something special next time out. So for now? Food court!

Think about what you spend. When you are with friends, that extra ten in your pocket can easily become change. But that ten added to other tens becomes the money you need for a car, the money you need for gas, the money for tickets to the hot concert of the summer.

Limit the money you carry with you. If you only have a certain amount to spend, you'll steer your friends—and yourself—to activities you can afford.

You may need to "take a loan" from your parents for a big expense—your Spanish class trip to Mexico—and then pay them back. Before you do this, write out and sign a loan agreement, and make sure you have a job set up or another way to get the money to pay back the loan.

Try to keep a budget. Keep it easy and simple. Savings and income in one column. Expenses in the other. Make sure you record all your expenses. If you are spending too much, figure out where to cut back or how to earn more.

CAR LOVE

Why is having a car—or at least knowing how to drive—so important?

I lived a half an hour away from my high school and the rest of civilization, so it was very important for me to have a car. My parents, though, didn't let me get one immediately, and I had my permit for ten months before I got my license and a car. Now I could never imagine a life without driving. Most of my friends lived anywhere from a half hour to over an hour away from me, so I rarely got to visit some of them before I could drive. Also, having a job without a car or knowing how to drive is almost impossible (especially if you're like me and get up for work at 5:30 in the morning). I actually hate to drive and would love nothing more than to have my parents drive me around, but sadly, we don't seem to have the same schedules, and I doubt that they would enjoy picking me up at my friend's house at one in the morning as much as they would be about dropping me off at work the next day before six in the morning. I also had to pay for my own car, which I think is very important to do, because I feel that the kids who buy their own car tend to have more respect about the whole overall aspect of driving as well as the responsibility of it than the kids whose parents gave them a car.

Life shouldn't totally revolve around your car. In my high school, what you drove was always a big deal, but when you go to college without your car, no one cares what you drive. ,,

—WHITNEY, 19

Car-Buying Tips. Along with advice on driving safety on page 180, Danny McKeever, owner of Fast Lane Racing School, offers some tips for buying your first car: "Almost all newer cars are pretty decent in terms of safety. I would recommend you buy a car with an antilock braking system, which takes the panic out of braking; air bags, of course; and traction control if offered. But remember, no amount of safety systems can overcome really bad, incompetent driving."

Car Costs. You may really want a car, but can you afford to own one? A car is not just the purchase price. You have to think about insurance, registration, plates, maintenance, and gas. Owning a car is a big expense and may take away money you want to spend on other things or that you need for your senior year or college. You may even find that you need to get a job just to pay for all the car expenses. So try using the business tools on pages 173 and 175 first. You may discover that borrowing your parents' car or taking the bus or even foot power is a smarter choice for you—for now.

You are managing your money and your time. How well are you managing one of the hardest parts of being a teen—pressures from friends? The next chapter will give you real tools to use when the pressure's on you.

Safe Driving: Advice from a Pro

Danny McKeever owns the Fast Lane Racing School and Fast Lane Teen Academy (fastlaneteenacademy.com). A champion race, stunt, and test car driver, he has won even more fame teaching others to win races and drive safely. His clients span the world of racing and celebrity: Cameron Diaz, Coolio, Josh Brolin, Tim Allen, George Lucas, Jay Leno, Picabo Street, Ashley Judd, Melissa Joan Hart, and many others. Danny says, "Police reports show 82 percent of teen accidents are caused by driver error." Here are his driving tips.

Many schools no longer offer driver's ed. And even if you are in one that does and you pass your road test, that doesn't mean you know how to avoid an accident or control a car.

You need to learn accident avoidance. Know your car's limits. Keep your eyes up, look ahead, and understand traction and tire management. If you drive too fast for the road conditions, you'll go out of control. A race car driver doesn't give up if a car spins out ahead of him. He steers around it. You shouldn't give up either.

Teens can learn practical skills and techniques—and hopefully, they'll never have to use the ones needed to avoid an accident. But if they do, here are eight important driving tips:

1. Driving is one of the few things you'll do in life where you have to pay 100 percent attention to what you are doing. Yes, 100 percent. Friends in your car will distract you—the more friends, the more distracted you'll be. Until you learn how to deal with having others in the car, drive with an adult or on your own.
2. Cars don't crash. People do. You can learn all the techniques in the world, but if you aren't in the right state of mind (calm and focused, not angry or upset), they're not going to be a big help.
3. A professional race car driver spends days finding the perfect seating position. Sit properly. Arms and legs should be bent

slightly. Hold the steering wheel with two hands. Sit high enough to see over the hood.

4. Look out at the big picture. Don't focus only on the car in front of you.
5. Wear your safety belt—always.
6. Never drive impaired—no driving after drinking alcohol, but also no driving when sleepy or on cold medication. You have to be alert.
7. Driving is like getting to an office being ready to work; you need to be ready to drive when you get into a car.
8. Clear out the clutter. No junk on the dashboard or stuff hanging from the visor. Make sure the windshield is clean and smear-free.

The Pressure's On

9

STAY TRUE TO YOU

> " We started a SADD chapter at our school and we have twenty-five peer counselors. We not only are trained to help the kids who come to us but also have become a huge support group for each other. "
>
> —RAYNA, 17

No one ever said high school was easy. Every day you face dilemmas and situations where your values and ability to make healthy choices are put to the test. In this chapter, a group of freshmen students at Stanford University give some advice on how they survived their high school years. Then Stephen Wallace, the chairman and chief executive officer of SADD National (Students Against Destructive Decisions, formerly known as Students Against Drunk Driving), offers his perspective.

Why are we afraid of popular people who do stupid things or make bad choices? Why do people kiss up to people you really can't respect? It doesn't make sense if you think about it.

—RITA, 13

I Survived High School—So Can You

Dr. Nancy Brown, a researcher at the Palo Alto Medical Foundation Research Institute (pamf.org/teen), answers teens' and preteens' health questions online, studies teen and preteen health issues, and teaches at Stanford University. She asked her college freshmen class on adolescent health four questions that reflected on their recent high school experiences. Here's what they had to say:

1. **What can you do to be true to yourself and not succumb to unhealthy media messages?**

I think many teens start smoking and drinking because of what they see on TV. They see a party scene in a movie and associate fun with drinking and smoking.

—CATHY

Our daily lives are so saturated by the media, and we are raised to view ourselves on the basis of what others see that we become accustomed to them, and when we get into high school, we feel like they've been around forever. "

—ELENI

" A sort of group consciousness is created in which everyone buys the same clothes, starts drinking, has to smoke. Everyone wants to fit in, so you need a strong self-image to avoid those pressures. "

—HAYLEY

" Being a teen is inherently stressful. Your body, emotions, and your life can seem out of control. The reality, though, is that the more time you spend being like everyone else, the less time you have to show the world why you are special. "

—MARIE

" You need to reflect on what you really want and who you really are. Set boundaries before you get in situations. Think about issues before you encounter them. "

—ANDREA

> Recognize that what you see in the media isn't real life. The media does not generally show the consequences of unhealthy behavior.

—REED

> Teens also have to realize that the media is promoting consumption. You think buying certain clothes or smoking a certain brand of cigarettes will make you cooler, more attractive, more sociable, or simply [able to] get a better-looking guy. It's so hard to be true to yourself because it's hard to say to your friends, 'I don't drink, and I am confident and comfortable about that.'

—NGAI-CHI

2. **If your friends are heavy drinkers or if you feel to be popular you have to have sex, drink, or take other unhealthy risks, what can you do?**

> I think you have to decide that being popular isn't your goal. Popularity doesn't mean you'll be happy. Saying no to friends isn't a crime. If you are in a situation where everyone is drinking and you don't want to, volunteer to be the designated driver, or say you can't sleep over and drive yourself home. There are several ways to get out of doing things you don't want to do without looking uncool.

—JENNY

" I was friends with 'cool' kids—I was homecoming queen—but if I was handed a drink, I'd just put it back. No big deal. "

—KRISTA

" You can blame your parents, sports the next day, practice on the weekend, 'my older brother will find out and kill me,' 'my older brother messed himself out, and now I can't get away with anything,' or if you are secure, 'I've got grand plans, and I'm not going to mess them up for one night of sex, drugs, or drinking.' "

—NICOLE

" Growing up in a different culture, drinking did not have the same connotations—drinking alcohol could be as simple as a glass of wine at the weekend *asado* (barbecue)—but I was often offered cigarettes and simply shook my head no. If a good friend offered me one, I'd make fun of them for smoking! "

—MARCELA

" Are your friends who are pressuring you the best people to have in your life? Friends who are really friends will respect your decisions. "

—CHRISTOPHER

> ❝ It's hard because you feel like you are letting the party mood down when you say no, but you can't do things you don't want to. You have to get to the point where if people think you're unpopular because you don't drink, then that's gonna have to be okay. ❞

—ANGELA

3. How important is it to be popular?

> ❝ When you get to college, you'll see being popular is really unimportant. And the 'nerds' in high school often wind up having the best jobs and making the most money! ❞

—HAYLEY

> ❝ Who knows what is 'popular'? No one. Make your own 'popular.' Be proud of who you are. ❞

—KRISTA

> ❝ Deep down, popularity was pretty important to me in high school. But I was able to put up a front like I didn't care if I fit in, but I did. There's a fine line between being yourself to be popular and being someone else. Once that line is crossed, you lose a sense of your own identity and make unhealthy decisions. To me, being popular isn't about the number of friends you have or how many people you slept with or how many shots

you took last night. Being popular is about the relationship you have with yourself and your own circle of friends. **"**

—JENNY

4. What are some ways to define success in high school?

" To be able to say, 'This is *me*: not-skinny, non-drinker, non-smoker.' But I don't think I was actually able to say that until I got to college, so try to define who you are and not who you are compared with others. **"**

—ANGELA

" What's important to you? If college, then good grades, extracurricular activities, doing well on tests. Sports? Did you give it your all? If you learn how to be an independent, responsible adult, making mistakes along the way, you are a success. **"**

—NICOLE

" Success could be looking back without regrets. Success is not defined by numbers, letters, or even other people. Success is being able to smile about where you are now. **"**

—KRISTA

Five Ways to Love You

Kelly White, executive editor at GL,
has some advice on "loving yourself."

1. **Keep it real.** Sounds cliché, sure, but you really do need to
   be true to you. It's okay and normal to be influenced by others,
   but don't let people sway you when you know, deep down in
   your heart of hearts, that it just isn't right. Whether it's a group
   of kids offering you a smoke or your BFF wanting you to join the
   chess club because the team needs one more player (but you'd
   rather be onstage performing under the spotlight), go with your
   gut. Only you know what's truly best for yourself.

2. **Pick positive people for pals.** Choose your friends wisely.
   Hanging out with kids who aren't on the right track can be
   destructive. Even if you're sticking to Rule No. 1 (above) and
   being conscious of making the right choices for yourself, associ-
   ating with the wrong people can cause you to be less than motivated. You should befriend energetic, conscientious gals and
   guys who will inspire you as much as you inspire them.

3. **Do sports.** Sign up for swim lessons, take up skiing, try out for
   soccer. Not only is staying active great for your physical health,
   but studies have proved that it does a major number on your
   self-esteem as well. Girls and guys who participate in sports do
   better in school and are less likely to use drugs and alcohol. Two
   added bonuses: being active releases endorphins (happy
   hormones!) in your brain, and it gets your body in its absolute
   best shape.

4. **Work your brain.** You might find this hard to believe, but your
   brain needs exercise, too. Yes, you get your fair share of mental
   workout while at school, but don't neglect your thinking muscle
   during weekends and summers. Figure out the ways you like to
   challenge yourself, and make it a point to feed your mind: do
   crossword puzzles, play video games that involve strategy, and

read, read, read. Whether you're into magazines, comic books, or paperback mysteries, discover the value of reading for pleasure. Nothing works that thinker the way reading does.

5. **Help others.** Nothing can get you feeling better about yourself than reaching out to people in need. You could volunteer to walk pups at the animal shelter (furry friends need love, too), tutor little kids who are struggling with fractions (you're a math whiz!), or help your elderly neighbor keep her lawn well groomed. You'll feel all sunshiny inside knowing you did your part to make the world just a little bit better. Oh, and be sure to look into how you can turn your good deeds into fulfilling your community service requirements at school. (For more on volunteering, see pages 197–201.)

DR. BROWN ADDS HER THOUGHTS

Dr. Brown, the researcher and teacher who asked the questions, has some thoughts on what teens experience: "The media images we all see are extremely distorted—there is very little reality out there for teens to compare yourselves against. Add to that our consumerism culture, where we think we can buy a product to fix anything and want quick fixes to anything that vexes us, and voilà, we have people molding themselves to meet those unhealthy media images. My advice is that there is always someone out there who will like what you like, enjoy spending time the way you do, or who will appreciate your sense of humor. Be brave—learn to start conversations with people you think you might have something in common with. Find strength in yourself, live up to your commitments, value yourself, do your best, look forward to things, respect other people, establish intimate relationships, and let yourself act like a fool with someone you love. Then you are coming close to being successful."

> **When you get into eleventh and twelfth grade, getting good grades and choosing your college become more important than going to parties and being popular.**
>
> —RAYNA, 17

Do Things That Are Extraordinary

Karen Bokram, Baltimore's 2005 Entrepreneur of the Year and the publisher and founding editor of *GL*, says, "Don't sit back and admire the view. Finish high school. Go to the best college you can. Pursue something that really interests you. If not college, find a more non-traditional path, like the arts. Think about what you need to reward and enrich yourself. Learn to do more with what you have. If you get to the point that you are recognized as a success, do something extraordinary."

> **When I was younger, I used to wear glasses, had a ponytail, and wore kind of plain clothes, and girls called me a geek. Over the summer, I ditched the clothes, glasses, and ponytail, and those same girls were like, 'Oh, gosh, you look great.' The attention made me feel good for a minute or so, but then I realized I shouldn't have to change how I look to get attention. I should just be me.**
>
> —BONNIE, 13

I was shocked when I got to high school—how much kids did drugs. People I knew were doing weed, lines of cocaine, heroin, acid . . . They start with weed and look for something more dangerous—to talk about and show off. They think they fit in by doing it, but they don't. Alcohol is a big deal, too. I've heard kids joke about driving and drinking—even after a whole year of health class and learning about the effects of drugs and alcohol and driving accidents. That impacted me and some of my friends but not everyone. You have to know where you stand, so you don't make wrong decisions. **"**

—HEATHER, 18

" Popularity can mean different things. Being popular because you throw yourself at guys isn't really popular, is it? If you are popular because you are a genuine person who people like being around, then you are really popular. **"**

—KELSEY, 16

When teens were being interviewed for this book, popularity—and how to define it—came up again and again. We hope this chapter helped you see that the best route to popularity is staying true to yourself.

Making Healthy Choices

Research by SADD (Students Against Destructive Decisions) with the Liberty Mutual Group found that what teens and their friends feel about themselves plays a significant role in whether they choose to drink or take drugs and make other unhealthy choices. Stephen Wallace, SADD's chairman and chief executive officer, travels the country speaking with teens and listening closely to what they have to say. He offers five action steps to help you make good lifestyle choices.

1. **Educate yourself about the real risks of destructive choices.**
   What are all the risks of a destructive choice you make?
   Impaired driving, drugs, underage drinking, bullying, early sexual behavior—all have social, emotional, legal, and physical risks. If you have sex, you don't just risk getting an STD, you also have emotional risks of being involved in a relationship you are too young to handle. If you drive drunk, you not only lose your driver's license but also may get a police record that could prevent you from getting into the college you want or getting the job you want.

2. **Tell your parents about the real world you live in.** Let them know the decisions you have to make every day, and find out what their expectations are. Your parents are the main reason you make good choices. SADD research shows that there is a reality gap: parents don't know about all the choices you have to make daily—what you are exposed to and how often you need to say no or avoid situations.

3. **Understand the myths that drive destructive decisions.** Don't believe the myth of inevitability—that all kids your age drink, smoke, have sex. SADD research shows that teens always over-report. So even if you read a study in a magazine or hear something on TV that says 63 percent of high school students drink, that also means that 37 percent don't, and even more aren't drinking every weekend and getting drunk. Look for those who

are making good choices. Also don't believe the myth of invincibility: that you're young, so you're indestructible. Poor choices have real and dangerous consequences. You can get maimed or killed if you drive drunk, or you might do the same to someone else. You can get AIDS from sexual activity. Bad things do happen.

4. **Look for a peer group that shares your values.** Look for friends who are positive. If you hang out with the wrong peer group, you will make wrong choices. If you are involved in something like community service, you're less likely to be bored. If your life is stressful, you are more likely to drink to relieve stress. Look for challenges and friends that support you.

5. **Plan ahead.** Think what decisions you'll be required to make, and decide what you'll do. Rehearse what you'll say—to yourself or with your family. Always have an out. Teens have said that they secretly are relieved there will be a breathalyzer at the prom because it gives them the excuse they need not to drink. For example, a high school boy told me he had a code with his parents. If he was in a situation that was getting out of hand, he could say that his grandma was sick and he'd promised to call home to see how she was doing. His parents knew that if he called them and asked, "How's Grandma?" that meant they needed to come and get him, and he would, in turn, tell the group that he needed to go, as his grandmother had gotten worse. Teens have told me that what they want is for their parents to help them make hard decisions and to stay up until they get home and enforce a curfew—help take the decision-making burden off of them. (See pages 186–88 for the excuses the students at Stanford used.) If you make a plan, you can develop a reputation that you don't drink and don't do drugs, and life will get easier as others will respect that. Think about what you want to be remembered for. Getting wasted every Friday? The kid having group sex on the bus? Or for honesty and sticking by your values? Who do you want to be?

Above and Beyond

10

> " I think one person can make big changes, but many people working together can truly make a huge difference. "
>
> —KARLY, 14

Volunteering may seem like one more thing that eats into your day. You know you have to do it to polish your résumé and your college application, but who really has the time? And what difference can one person make?

> " Don't ask what the world needs. Ask what makes you come alive, and go do it. Because what the world needs is people who have come alive. "
>
> —HOWARD THURMAN, AMERICAN THEOLOGIAN, CLERGYMAN, AND ACTIVIST, 1900–1981

When you volunteer, you:

> Give back
> Find yourself
> Learn about others
> Let others know you are ready to make a meaningful contribution
> Build skills
> Enter the real world

Okay, so you've decided that you have the interest and ability to engage in action in your community. The next step is figuring out how to use those interests and abilities to meet real community needs. There are probably a number of places right in your own neighborhood that can match your skills with community needs:

> The United Way (unitedway.org) in many communities serves as a sort of umbrella organization for local service agencies and often also serves as a clearinghouse for formal and informal opportunities for people in the community to work with these agencies.
> Your local chapter of the Hands On Network (handsonnetwork .org) also works to connect community members with opportunities to become involved by actually coordinating group volunteer projects that anyone can sign up for.
> Check with your teachers, guidance counselor, or community service director to see if your school offers or is interested in developing service-learning classes.
> Places of worship in your community like mosques, synagogues, and churches often have a really good sense of the needs of your particular community and can connect you directly with opportunities to serve.
> Check with your city hall or municipal building to learn about opportunities to lend a youth perspective to community issues at city council meetings or as part of a youth board.

Action Without Borders

Trish Tchume is the campus organizer of Action Without Borders/Idealist.org. She has a lot to say about the value of volunteerism:

Why make a community connection? What's the point? What's the benefit? So, you're a citizen of your community, nation, world—what exactly does that mean? What is your role?

A friend of mine who works as a volunteer coordinator in Philadelphia has a wonderful quote on her office wall by an Aboriginal woman named Lilla Watson. It says, "If you have come to help me, you are wasting your time. But if you have come because your liberation is bound up with mine, then let us work together." This saying really speaks to my own experiences with community. Over the years, I've come to realize how greatly our choices, however seemingly large or small, impact those around us as well as those throughout the world. Knowing this, Lilla's words serve to remind me that when I choose to "help" others through activities such as volunteering, I'm not only working for the benefit of others, I'm also working toward my own personal goals of a more just and respectful world.

Action Without Borders/Idealist.org (idealist.org) was built upon this simple idea that ordinary people have the power to build a better world; they often just need to connect with other individuals, organizations, and resources that can support them in their efforts. In my work as a campus organizer for Action Without Borders/Idealist.org, I have the privilege of sharing this idea with young people on a daily basis. During these interactions, my primary objective is always to convey the message that most of us already possess the key ingredients for effecting positive social change. It simply takes one part ability to recognize both problems and opportunities, one part knowledge of available resources, and two parts willingness to do what it takes to bring all of these ingredients together!

Other Ways to Get Connected

Here are some other organizations that focus on helping teens to get involved in their communities:

➤ Taking IT Global, takingitglobal.org
➤ Do Something, dosomething.org
➤ Youth Service America, ysa.org
➤ Youth Venture, youthventure.org

Youth organizations, both national (such as Boys and Girls Clubs, Girls Inc., Campfire, Girl Scouts, and Boy Scouts) and state or local, offer opportunities to take action in communities all around the country. And some organizations offer well-recognized awards, such as the Girl Scout Gold Award or the Boy Scout Eagle Award, for taking on a project that affects the community in a major way.

Action Without Borders/Idealist.org has also developed a great website just for kids and teens who are looking for ways to get involved. The kids and teens site includes the following information:

➤ At the Volunteer Resource Center (idealist.org/kt/index.html), you can search a huge online database for actual volunteer opportunities anywhere in the world or right in your own backyard.
➤ A page of links directs you to organizations started by kids just like you who saw a problem and decided to do something about it (idealist.org/kt/youthorgs.html).
➤ For those who are also interested in learning more about a particular issue of concern, a page titled "World Around You" (idealist.org/kt/ktorgsearch.html) offers links to organizations with issue-specific information geared to young people.

➤ If you're not finding a group or an organization that's working on an issue you think is important, the kids and teens site offers a page of resources on how to turn your own ideas into action (idealist.org/kt/activism.html).

These ideas are only the beginning. The potential you have to work for a better world is boundless. Your role now is to determine which issues matter most to you and make the decision of where, when, and how to devote your energy to these issues.

> As I looked down, I saw a large river meandering slowly along for miles, passing from one country to another without stopping. I also saw huge forests, extending along several borders. And I watched the extent of one ocean touch the shores of separate continents. Two words leaped to mind as I looked down on all this: commonality and interdependence. We are one world.

—JOHN-DAVID BARTOE, ASTRONAUT

School of Dreams

One November, the teens in the youth group at Lyall Memorial Federated Church in Millbrook, New York, were looking through store catalogs and listing what they wanted for Christmas. Flip phone, iPod, Xbox, PlayStation, sneakers, jeans—but the leader, Maggie Blayney, had slipped in another catalog. With its snowy scene, it looked like all the others, but inside were "gifts" you could buy for other people, not yourself. The catalog, called Samaritan's Purse, had descriptions of "food for a hungry family of five for a week," "life-saving surgery for one child," "a dozen chickens," "a blanket," "fresh water for a year," "medicine for a small village." Silence fell over the room. Everyone had been asking for luxuries, but here were people

Using Your Power

Trish Tchume offers some ideas on using your power.

What kind of power do you have? As an individual? As part of a group? What are some ways to use that power? For good? For change?

You have enormous power both as a group member and as an individual. Here are just a few examples of the many ways that you can especially harness that power to bring about positive social change.

Peer Pressure

Peer pressure is such a dreaded term—often used in reference to the power that young people have to get their peers to engage in activities that might hurt them. But peer pressure isn't always a negative thing! Through your very own words and actions, you can influence your peers to recognize and positively address some of the biggest issues facing our world today.

And now more than ever, there are so many ways to let people know that you're ready and willing to work for what you believe in. You can voice your concerns with a T-shirt, create a zine that gives your friends a space to talk about their interests, post your opinions on a blog, or send an e-mail to the editor of your school or local newspaper, to name a few. The possibilities are endless!

Power of the Purse

Young people can make a huge impact with their spending dollars. Don't appreciate the way that a store treats its employees? Annoyed by the negative way a singer on the radio talks about women? You can reflect your displeasure or support by choosing to boycott or purchase certain products. Everyone from manufacturers to retailers to entertainers knows how important it is for them to cater to your interests, so you can speak volumes by choosing to open or close your wallet.

Get Politically Involved

"But I can't even vote!" Voting is definitely one of the greatest tools that people can use to add their voices to the social conversation. But what if you're not old enough to vote? Do you have to wait until you're 18 before your opinions carry any weight? No way! There's no minimum age requirement to contact your elected officials. You can also talk to people who *are* old enough to vote about the issues that are important to you and encourage them to consider these issues when *they* vote.

Power of the Pen

If you're old enough to write a letter, you already have the power to save a life. Every day, in countries all over the world, people just like you and me are unfairly imprisoned and even tortured for speaking up about injustice. Humanitarian organizations like Amnesty International (amnestyusa.org/youth/) link average citizens young and old with the basic tools necessary to potentially save the lives of these prisoners of conscience. As hard as it may be to believe, even at your age, your ability to write a letter of support on behalf of these individuals can make all the difference in the world.

---

yearning for life's basic needs: clean water, enough food, shelter, health. The kids had been studying a passage from the Bible: "Don't live any longer the way this world lives. Let your way of thinking be completely changed."

Somebody saw a description in the catalog, "Build a school in Afghanistan for $3,500." Their own community had just raised funds for a new high school that would benefit these kids. But here was a community with no school, where girls until recently had been unable even to go to school. Could they raise enough money to build a school in Afghanistan? The School of Dreams was born.

Within one year of much hard work, the group raised $5,500— $2,000 over the $3,500 needed—so that each of the Afghani students could get the new school and be equipped with school supplies. People like you learned that Afghanistan had six thousand schools before the war and all had been damaged. Everyone pledged half of all the money he or she made doing chores for community residents. All through the year, the teens washed windows, mowed lawns, baby-sat, and shoveled snow. They created handmade Christmas ornaments and set up a table, caroling to attract attention and giving an ornament to anyone who donated. They raised $450 in two hours and, with additional community donations, exceeded their goal. The group hopes that once the school is operational, they can have a pen-pal relationship with the students. "The group gained a real sense of what they could accomplish by working together," said Maggie Blayney. (Additional information courtesy of The Millbrook Roundtable and Rebecca Whalen, staff reporter.)

Think of what you could do with a group!

> How wonderful it is that nobody need wait a single moment before starting to improve the world.
>
> —ANNE FRANK

Your Spiritual Side

Many people start to question their spiritual beliefs during the high school years. Your church, synagogue, mosque, or other house of worship becomes an obligation left over from childhood. Where once you enjoyed the ritual and the feeling of peace you gained by attending services, you now value much more highly your extra hours of sleep. You may still go to keep your parents from complaining, but what do you get from your beliefs?

Questioning Is Healthy

Rick Beckwith has served on the Young Life, a non-denominational Christian organization for middle and high school kids, staff for over twenty years in numerous different roles. He has consulted with leaders in France, England, Germany, Italy, and the United States to discern how best to encourage teenagers to achieve success and fulfillment in life. In 1999, he consulted with the Institute for Classical Achievement to help them develop and teach their Start Smart Program geared to help graduating high school seniors prepare to succeed in college. What does he have to say about questioning spiritual beliefs?

Most kids question their spiritual beliefs during adolescence. And if they don't, they should be encouraged to, because it will make them stronger down the road. Early adolescents are beginning to break away from their parents and form the identities they will carry as adults. So they try on different personality traits to see what works for them. The ones they like, they keep. The ones they don't, they discard and try something else.

The same is true with their faith. Early adolescents should be encouraged to question the faith of their upbringing. Honestly working through doubts or difficulties with knowledgeable adults or youth leaders can help you to come to find a personal faith you can call your own. This faith can help when you are jilted by a friend, cut from a sports team, or have parents going through a divorce.

If you are looking for something to believe in, find some people whose lives you respect, and see what makes them tick. Peer support is so important. Getting plugged into a youth group is helpful, as is having friends with similar values.

> " I do believe in God. It gets me through things when I pray . . . like sometimes it helps me have more patience—especially with my little brothers. "
>
> —AMY, 15

What's Next in Your Life?

You may look back at your high school years with nostalgia and go to every reunion, or you may simply be glad you got through those four years and never look back, or you may fit someplace in between. If this book is your guide to succeeding in all the ways that matter in high school, then you can also use it to prepare you for what's next: college, work, career, more committed relationships—all the steps to adulthood.

> " I was very closed-minded in high school. In college, I opened my mind—ready to meet new people and try new things. College is a time to experience life, get out on your own, find your potential. I go to a college that doesn't tell me what clothes to wear, what to believe, or who to be friends with. It's wonderful to just breathe and be myself. "
>
> —WHITNEY, 19

When you're growing up, your mother says, 'Wear boots, or you'll catch cold.' When you become an adult, you discover that you have the right to not wear boots and to see if you catch cold or not. It's something like that.

—DIANE ARBUS, AMERICAN PHOTOGRAPHER

I really don't think life is about the I-could-have-beens. Life is only about the I-tried-to-do. I don't mind the failure, but I can't imagine that I'd forgive myself if I didn't try.

—NIKKI GIOVANNI, AMERICAN POET

Let's hope that this book has given you the tools you need to make smart choices about relationships, your health, school, jobs, money, and time. Have you thought about where you are going? And how you will get there? Have you connected with your community? Learned to take care of yourself? Discovered what you value in a relationship? Figured out how to stay true to you? Then you are on your way to one of the greatest benefits of being an adult: using your independence and freedom responsibly to benefit yourself, those close to you, and your community, your society, and the world.